Southwest Missouri S

FIFTH EDITION
MANAGEMENT

STEPHEN P.
ROBBINS

MARY
COULTER

PRENTICE HALL, Upper Saddle River, N.J. 07458

> This Study Guide is dedicated
> to Sue Feltes Miller
> for her humor, patience and intelligence.

Production manager: Richard Bretan
Acquisions editor: David Shafer
Associate editor: Lisamarie Brassini
Manufacturing buyer: Ken Clinton

 © 1996 by Prentice-Hall, Inc.
A Simon & Schuster Company
Upper Saddle River, NJ 07458

All rights reserved. No part of this book may be reproduced, in any form or by any means, without permission in writing from the publisher.

Printed in the United States of America

10 9 8 7 6 5 4 3 2 1

ISBN 0-13-486655-X

Prentice-Hall International (UK) Limited, *London*
Prentice-Hall of Australia Pty. Limited, *Sydney*
Prentice-Hall Canada, Inc., *Toronto*
Prentice-Hall Hispanoamericana, S.A., *Mexico*
Prentice-Hall of India Private Limited, *New Delhi*
Prentice-Hall of Japan, Inc., *Tokyo*
Simon & Schuster Asia Pte. Ltd., *Singapore*
Editora Prentice-Hall do Brazil, Ltda., *Rio de Janeiro*

CONTENTS

Preface

Suggested Study Approach

Chapter 1	MANAGERS AND MANAGEMENT	1
Chapter 2	THE EVOLUTION OF MANAGEMENT	10
Chapter 3	ORGANIZATIONAL CULTURE AND ENVIRONMENT: THE CONSTRAINTS	19
Chapter 4	MANAGING IN A GLOBAL ENVIRONMENT	27
Chapter 5	SOCIAL RESPONSIBILITY AND MANAGERIAL ETHICS	35
Chapter 6	DECISION MAKING: THE ESSENCE OF THE MANAGER'S JOB	45
Chapter 7	FOUNDATIONS OF PLANNING	56
Chapter 8	STRATEGIC MANAGEMENT	65
Chapter 9	PLANNING TOOLS AND TECHNIQUES	76
Chapter 10	ORGANIZATION STRUCTURE AND DESIGN	87
Chapter 11	HUMAN RESOURCE MANAGEMENT	97
Chapter 12	MANAGING CHANGE AND INNOVATION	108
Chapter 13	FOUNDATIONS OF BEHAVIOR	118
Chapter 14	UNDERSTANDING GROUPS AND TEAMS	128
Chapter 15	MOTIVATING EMPLOYEES	138
Chapter 16	LEADERSHIP	150
Chapter 17	COMMUNICATION AND INTERPERSONAL SKILLS	160
Chapter 18	FOUNDATIONS OF CONTROL	172
Chapter 19	OPERATIONS MANAGEMENT	181
Chapter 20	CONTROL TOOLS AND TECHNIQUES	191

Answers for Objective Questions　　　　　　　　　　　　　　　　203

PREFACE

This Study Guide has been designed to supplement <u>Management</u>, fifth edition, by Stephen P. Robbins and Mary Coulter. The purpose of this Study Guide is to aid in your understanding of the text material.

Each chapter of the Student Study Guide contains the objectives of the chapter, an outline of the material, and a listing of key terms and their definitions. The key terms section is also outlined when appropriate to put together those items which are subterms of key words. In addition, three sections of questions are included to help you understand the concepts of management more fully. Questions include Multiple-choice, True/False, and a section of Matching terms with definitions.

SUGGESTED STUDY APPROACH

Management is an exciting, important, and universal activity. Steve Robbins and Mary Coulter, the authors of this textbook, have tried to convey their enthusiasm for the subject as well as the factual content to you, the future managers of United States business. Hopefully, as you progress through the management text you will become fascinated about how organizations are managed and challenged to use your knowledge to make that management even more effective.

Students should read the text material first, paying close attention to the Learning Objectives at the beginning of each chapter. Be sure to pay special attention to the key words and definitions in the margin of the page. Students often find that the language in a course of study can be difficult or confusing particularly when it is the first course in a subject. Words that you may consider part of your normal vocabulary can have very specific or even different meanings.

Be aware of how the material is divided. The headings and subheadings of the chapter help to organize the information. Notice which sections build on or are derived from others. There are numerous tables, graphs, and charts to help illustrate the concepts.

Don't neglect the boxed sections. They add real world examples and a discussion of issues. Sometimes it's easy to forget why you are studying management when a test is getting close and there are so many things to remember. The interviews with practicing managers are a great way to remind you that you will be using the things you've learned in the classroom when you are the practicing manager.

After reading the chapter, review the Summary section at the end of the material. Try answering the Review Questions which follow. You will notice that they are tied to the objectives stated at the beginning of the chapter.

When you have covered the material in the chapter, turn to this Study Guide. Review the objectives at the beginning of each section. Read through the chapter outline, mentally expanding on the information you remember from the text itself. Then answer the multiple choice, true/false, and matching questions. Be fair to yourself and don't glance back at the material while taking the test. The answers to the questions will be found at the end of this Study Guide.

Don't stop studying just because you've completed the study guide questions. Review the material you answered incorrectly. Is there a pattern in your errors. Are you having a problem with a particular concept or definitions in general or have you shortchanged some area of the chapter when you were reading it. Even if you get all the answers correct - Bravo! - remember that not every possible question was included so your professor may think of some others that are not found in this guide. Go back to the text and go through the material again with a double dose of studying anything you didn't do well on in the sample questions.

CHAPTER 1

MANAGERS AND MANAGEMENT

Chapter Objectives

1. Differentiate managers from operatives.

2. Define management.

3. Distinguish between effectiveness and efficiency.

4. Describe the four basic management functions.

5. Identify the roles performed by managers.

6. Describe the skills managers need.

7. Explain whether or not the manager's job is generic.

8. Explain the value of studying management.

Chapter Outline

I. Who are Managers?

    A. What are Organizations?

        1. Characteristics of Organizations

        2. Organizational Levels

II. What is Management and What do Managers Do?

    A. Defining Management.

    B. Efficiency and Effectiveness

    C. Management Functions

D. Management Roles

  1. Interpersonal Roles

  2. Informational Roles

  3. Decisional Roles

E. Management Skills

  1. Technical Skills

  2. Human Skills

  3. Conceptual Skills

F. Is the Manager's Job Universal?

  1. Organizational Level

  2. Organizational Type

  3. Organizational Size

  4. Cross-national Transferability

III. The Value the Marketplace Puts on Managers

IV. Why Study Management?

Key Terms

Organization - A systematic arrangement of people to accomplish some specific purpose.

Operatives - People who work directly on a job or task and have no responsibility for overseeing the work of others.

Managers - Individuals in an organization who direct the activities of others.

  First-line managers - Supervisors; the lowest level of management.

  Middle managers - All levels of management between the supervisory level and the top level of the organization.

  Top managers - Managers at or near the pinnacle of the organization who are responsible for making the decisions and setting the policies that affect all aspects of the organization.

Management - The process of getting activities completed efficiently and effectively with and through other people.

Efficiency - The relationship between inputs and outputs, seeks to minimize resource costs.

Effectiveness - Goal attainment.

Management Functions - Planning, Organizing, leading, and controlling.

>**Planning** - Includes defining goals, establishing strategy, and developing plans to coordinate activities.

>**Organizing** - Determining what tasks are to be done, who is to do them, how the tasks are to be grouped, who reports to whom, and where decisions are to be made.

>**Leading** - Includes motivating subordinates, directing others, selecting the most effective communication channels, and resolving conflicts.

>**Controlling** - Monitoring activities to ensure that they are being accomplished as planned and correcting any significant deviations.

Management Roles - Specific categories of managerial behavior.

>**Interpersonal roles** - Roles that include figurehead, leader, and liaison activities.

>**Informational roles** - Roles that include monitoring, disseminating, and spokesperson activities.

>**Decisional roles** - Roles that include those of entrepreneur, disturbance handler, resource allocator, and negotiator.

Management Skills

>**Technical skills** - Skills that include knowledge of and proficiency in a certain specialized field.

>**Human skills** - The ability to work well with other people both individually and in a group.

>**Conceptual skills** - The ability to think and to conceptualize about abstract situations, to see the organization as a whole and the relationships among its various subunits, and to visualize how the organization fits into its broader environment.

Small Business - An independently owned and operated profit-seeking enterprise having fewer than five hundred employees.

Entrepreneurship - A process by which people pursue opportunities, fulfilling needs and wants through innovation, without regard to the resources they currently control.

MULTIPLE CHOICE QUESTIONS

1. Determining what tasks need to be done and who is to do them is a part of

    a. planning.
    b. organizing.
    c. leading.
    d. controlling.

2. Comparing actual performance with previously set goals is a part of

    a. planning.
    b. organizing.
    c. leading.
    d. controlling.

3. Selecting the most effective communication channel for use among organization members is a part of

    a. planning.
    b. organizing.
    c. leading.
    d. controlling.

4. _____ studied five chief executives at work and identified ten managerial roles.

    a. Henri Fayol.
    b. Max Weber.
    c. Steve Smith.
    d. Henry Mintzberg.

5. Which is not a characteristic of an organization?

    a. An organization has a distinct purpose.
    b. An organization is composed of people.
    c. An organization always seeks to earn a profit.
    d. An organization has a structure that defines and limits people.

6. "Doing things right" describes

    a. effectiveness.
    b. leadership.
    c. efficiency.
    d. middle level managers.

7. _____ first wrote about the management functions.

    a. Henry Mintzberg
    b. Max Weber
    c. Michael Porter
    d. Henri Fayol

8. Establishing goals is a part of

    a. planning.
    b. organizing.
    c. leading.
    d. controlling.

9. Lisa Bradley is a professor who teaches at the local college. She is probably

    a. a top-manager.
    b. a middle manager.
    c. a first-line supervisor.
    d. an operative.

10. CEO Mike Warren from Alabama Gas Co. understands that_____ is key to effective leadership.

    a. involvement
    b. ethics
    c. status
    d. financial incentives

11. Operatives are

    a. people who manage others.
    b. first-line supervisors.
    c. middle managers.
    d. people who work directly on a job and have no managerial responsibility.

12. The three common characteristics of an organization include all of the following except

    a. distinct purpose.
    b. technology.
    c. people.
    d. systematic structure.

13. Which of the following characteristics is not one of those required to be a successful manager today?

    a. being a star player.
    b. being self reliant with a "bundle" of skills.
    c. be an expert or specialist at something.
    d. being a team player.

14. According to research, the small business manager's most important role is as a

    a. resource allocator.
    b. spokesperson
    c. monitor.
    d. disseminator.

15. Compared to traditional managers, entrepreneurs

    a. tend to be custodial.
    b. take little financial risk.
    c. are motivated by career promotions.
    d. are motivated by a desire for independence.

16. When the president of a university hands out diplomas at commencement, she/he is acting in the role of

    a. leader.
    b. figurehead.
    c. liaison.
    d. disseminator.

17. When CEO Marge Cohen holds Board meetings, she is acting in the role of

    a. disseminator.
    b. entrepreneur.
    c. figurehead.
    d. spokesperson.

18. Hal Holden is responsible for representing the organization when the union contract is being renegotiated. He is fulfilling the managerial role of

    a. disturbance handler.
    b. liaison.
    c. negotiator.
    d. spokesperson.

19. The informational roles of a manager include all of the following except

   a. figurehead.
   b. monitor.
   c. disseminator.
   d. spokesperson.

20. A manager distributes organizational resources like supplies and administrative dollars to departments is performing the role of

   a. resource allocator.
   b. monitor.
   c. disseminator.
   d. leader.

TRUE/FALSE QUESTIONS

1. T F   First-line managers are usually called supervisors.

2. T F   Management is a process of getting activities completed efficiently with and through other people.

3. T F   It is enough for managers to simply be efficient in carrying out their duties.

4. T F   Controlling is a process used to make sure an organization's actions are consistent with the organization's plans.

5. T F   It is usually not necessary for managers to perform all four management functions in carrying out their jobs.

6. T F   According to research, managers spend long periods of time doing reflective thinking about their work.

7. T F   It is more important to be efficient than effective.

8. T F   The management functions include planning, monitoring, organizing, and controlling.

9. T F   Managers have different orientations toward planning at different levels of the organization.

10. T F   When a manager is efficient, she/he is also being effective.

11. T F   Since management is a generic activity, a manager's work is the same regardless of what is managed.

12. T F   The roles of small and large business managers are basically the same.

13. T F   Management concepts are not generically transferable to international settings.

14. T F   One reason that management is an important topic of study for students is because every worker will either manage or be managed.

15. T F   A business is classified as small if it has fewer than 1000 employees.

MATCH TERMS WITH DEFINITIONS

a. Planning
b. Organizing
c. Leading
d. Controlling
e. Efficiency
f. Effectiveness
g. Interpersonal roles
h. Informational roles
i. Decisional roles
j. Technical skills
k. Human skills
l. Conceptual skills

___ 1. Skills that include knowledge of and proficiency in a certain specialized field.

___ 2. Roles that include monitoring, disseminating, and spokesperson activities.

___ 3. Includes motivating subordinates, directing others, selecting the most effective communication channels, and resolving conflicts.

___ 4. Determining what tasks are to be done, who is to do them, how the tasks are to be grouped, who reports to whom, and where decisions are to be made.

___ 5. Roles that include figurehead, leader and liaison activities.

___ 6. The ability to think and to conceptualize about abstract situations, to see the organization as a whole and the relationships among its various subunits, and to visualize how the organization fits into its broader environment.

___ 7. The ability to work well with other people both individually and in a group.

___ 8. Roles that include those of entrepreneur, disturbance handler, resource allocator, and negotiator.

___ 9. Goal attainment.

___ 10. The relationship between inputs and outputs, seeks to minimize resource costs.

___ 11. Includes defining goals, establishing strategy, and developing plans to coordinate activities.

___ 12. Monitoring activities to ensure that they are being accomplished as planned and correcting any significant deviations.

CHAPTER 2

THE EVOLUTION OF MANAGEMENT

Chapter Objectives

1. Explain the value of studying management history.

2. Identify some major pre-twentieth-century contributions to management.

3. Define Frederick Taylor's principles of scientific management.

4. Summarize scientific management's contribution to management.

5. Identify Henri Fayol's contributions to management.

6. Describe Max Weber's ideal bureaucracy.

7. Explain the contributions of the Hawthorne studies to management.

8. Contrast the approaches taken by human relations advocates and the behavioral science theorists.

9. Distinguish between the process, systems, and contingency approaches.

10. Describe how the following trends are impacting management practices: work force diversity, ethics, innovation and change, total quality management, re-engineering, empowerment and teams, the bimodal work force, downsizing, and contingent workers.

Chapter Outline

  I. Historical Background

 II. The Early Years

    A. Scientific Management

       1. Frederick Taylor

       2. Frank and Lillian Gilbreth

3. Henry Gantt

4. Putting Scientific Management into Perspective

B. General Administrative Theorists

1. Henri Fayol

2. Max Weber

3. Putting the General Administrative Theorists into Perspective

C. Human Resources Approach

1. Early Advocates

2. The Hawthorne Studies

3. The Human Relations Movement

4. Behavioral Science Theorists

5. Putting the Human Resources Contributors into Perspective

D. The Quantitative Approach

III. Recent Years: Toward Integration

A. The Process Approach

B. The Systems Approach

C. The Contingency Approach

IV. Current Trends and Issues

A. Workforce Diversity

B. Ethics

C. Stimulating Innovation and Change

D. Total Quality Management

E. Re-engineering

F. Empowerment and Teams

G. The Bimodal Workforce

H. Downsizing

I. Contingent Workers

Key Terms

Division of Labor - The breakdown of jobs into narrow, repetitive tasks.

Industrial Revolution - The advent of machine power, mass production, and efficient transportation.

Scientific Management - The use of the scientific method to define the "one best way" for a job to be done.

Therbligs - A classification scheme for labeling seventeen basic hand motions.

Gantt Chart - A graphic bar chart that shows the relationship between work planned and completed on one axis and time elapsed on the other.

General Administrative Theorists - Writers who developed general theories of what managers do and what constitutes good management practice.

Classical theorists - The term used to describe the scientific management theorists and general administrative theorists.

Principle of Management - Universal truths of management that can be taught in school.

Bureaucracy - A form of organization marked by division of labor, hierarchy, rules and regulations, and impersonal relationships.

Human Resources Approach - The study of management that focuses on human behavior.

Hawthorne Studies - A series of studies during the 1920s and 1930s that provided new insights in group norms and behavior.

Human Relations Movement - The belief, for the most part unsubstantiated by research, that a satisfied worker will be productive.

Behavioral Science Theorists - Psychologists and sociologists who relied on the scientific method for the study of organizational behavior.

Quantitative Approach - The use of quantitative techniques to improve decision making.

Process Approach - Management performs the functions of planning, organizing, leading, and controlling.

Systems Approach - A theory that sees an organization as a set of interrelated and interdependent parts.

Closed systems - Systems that neither are influenced by, nor interact with, their environment.

Open systems - Dynamic systems that interact with and respond to their environment.

Contingency Approach - Recognizing and responding to situational variables as they arise.

Workforce Diversity - Employees in organizations are heterogeneous in terms of gender, race, ethnicity, or other characteristics.

Total Quality Management (TQM) - A philosophy of management that is driven by customer needs and expectations.

Re-engineering - A radical redesign of all or part of a company's work processes to improve productivity and financial performance.

Empowerment - Increasing the decision-making discretion of workers.

Bimodal Workforce - Employees tend to perform either low-skilled service jobs for near-minimum wage or high-skilled well-paying jobs.

Downsizing - Organizational restructuring efforts in which individuals are laid off from their jobs.

Contingent Workers - Part-time, temporary, or freelance employees.

MULTIPLE CHOICE

1. The first major step toward developing a formal theory of management began

    a. with the Egyptian Pyramids and the Great Wall of China.
    b. in the early 1900s.
    c. after World War II.
    d. during the Industrial Revolution.

2. The person who developed the idea of teaching management principles in schools and universities was

    a. Frederick Taylor.
    b. Max Weber.
    c. Henri Fayol.
    d. Henry Gantt.

3. The person who developed a science for work by studying the movements required to move pig iron and the size of shovels used was

   a. Frederick Taylor.
   b. Max Weber.
   c. Henri Fayol.
   d. Henry Gantt.

4. The person who developed the idea for giving a bonus if a worker finished the assigned task for the day was

   a. Frederick Taylor.
   b. Max Weber.
   c. Henri Fayol.
   d. Henry Gantt.

5. The person who described the "ideal bureaucracy" was

   a. Frederick Taylor.
   b. Max Weber.
   c. Henri Fayol.
   d. Henry Gantt.

6. The person who described the management functions and fourteen principles of management was

   a. Frederick Taylor.
   b. Max Weber.
   c. Henri Fayol.
   d. Henry Gantt.

7. Robert Owen was a contributor to this historical era in management

   a. scientific management
   b. general administrative approach
   c. human resources approach
   d. quantitative approach

8. Marcy Harnes uses linear programming for decision making. She is benefitting from

   a. the scientific management approach.
   b. the human resources approach.
   c. the general administrative approach.
   d. the quantitative approach.

9. The use of industrial psychology was developed and popularized by the
    a. scientific management
    b. general administrative approach
    c. human resources approach
    d. quantitative approach

10. Therbligs were created by

    a. Frederick Taylor.
    b. Frank and Lillian Gilbreth.
    c. Max Weber.
    d. Robert Owen.

11. Which is not one of Mary Parker Follett's contributions to management study?

    a. Managers should rely on formal authority to lead workers.
    b. An organization should be based on a group ethic and not on individualism.
    c. Managers and workers are partners.
    d. The manager's job is to coordinate group efforts.

12. A common thread that united human relations supporters like Carnegie, Maslow, and McGregor was an unshakable optimism about

    a. the formal organization.
    b. authority.
    c. people's capabilities.
    d. group dynamics.

13. The process approach was originally introduced by

    a. Frederick Taylor.
    b. Henri Fayol.
    c. Robert Owen.
    d. Henry Gantt.

14. An integrative approach to management in which decisions are dependent on situational factors is the

    a. systems approach.
    b. process approach.
    c. contingency approach.
    d. quantitative approach.

15. An integrative approach which makes the external environment an important consideration is

    a. systems approach.
    b. process approach.
    c. contingency approach.
    d. all of the above.

16. Development of a unifying framework for management began in earnest

    a. after World War II.
    b. in the early 1980s.
    c. during the time of the Hawthorne Studies.
    d. in the early 1960s.

17. Scientific Management insisted there was only "one right way" to do a job and it was the manager's responsibility to tell the workers what that was. What current trend would dispute that view?

    a. bimodal work force.
    b. work force diversity.
    c. total quality management.
    d. empowerment.

18. James Herriott has been laid off from his skilled employment. He has taken a position with a local pet shop as a retail clerk. His wife is a highly paid attorney. Which current trend describes their situation?
    a. bimodal work force.
    b. work force diversity.
    c. total quality management.
    d. empowerment.

19. Maria Lopez is a hispanic who manages a production team consisting of Louise Smith, physically challenged Kerry Drake, Yan Lui, and Bob Jeffries. Which current trend describes their situation?

    a. bimodal work force.
    b. work force diversity.
    c. total quality management.
    d. empowerment.

20. Maria Lopez's team is given considerable discretion in how the production work should be organized. Which current trend describes their situation?

    a. bimodal work force.
    b. work force diversity.
    c. total quality management.
    d. empowerment.

TRUE/FALSE QUESTIONS

1. T F Management links together ideas and research findings from many diverse specializations such as psychology, sociology, and mathematics.

2. T F Four distinct approaches that explain the history of management include: scientific management, general administrative theory, the human resources approach, and the behavioral science approach.

3. T F Henri Fayol was a major contributor to the scientific approach to management.

4. T F Frederick Taylor wanted to create a mental revolution among both workers and managers by developing a science for work.

5. T F Bureaucracy is not unlike scientific management in its ideology because both emphasize rationality, predictability, impersonality, technical competence, and authoritarianism.

6. T F Both scientific management and general administrative theorists viewed organizations as machines.

7. T F The functional view of the manager's job owes its origin to Henri Fayol.

8. T F Robert Owen suggested the use of psychological test to improve employee selection.

9. T F The acceptance view of authority was developed by Max Weber.

10. T F The Hawthorne Studies consisted of several different experiments and lasted over a period of twelve years.

11. T F Organizations are open systems.

12. T F Some interdependent factors in an organization system include individuals, groups, attitudes, motives, formal structure, interactions, status, and authority.

13. T F The workforce is less heterogeneous than it was twenty years ago.

14. T F Managers today are often more effective when they coach and cheer their workers on than when they tell workers what to do.

15. T F Re-engineering refers to the minor adjustments good managers make to the ongoing organization.

MATCH TERMS WITH DEFINITIONS

a. Bimodal Workforce
b. Downsizing
c. Gantt Chart
d. Open systems
e. Closed systems
f. Total Quality Management
g. Re-engineering
h. Empowerment
i. Bureaucracy
j. Scientific Management
k. Therbligs
l. Division of Labor
m. Contingent Workers

___ 1. The use of the scientific method to define the "one best way" for a job to be done.

___ 2. A graphic bar chart that shows the relationship between work planned and completed on one axis and time elapsed on the other.

___ 3. A form of organization marked by division of labor, hierarchy, rules and regulations, and impersonal relationships.

___ 4. Systems that neither are influenced by, nor interact with, their environment.

___ 5. A radical redesign of all or part of a company's work processes to improve productivity and financial performance.

___ 6. Employees tend to perform either low-skilled service jobs for near-minimum wage or high-skilled well-paying jobs.

___ 7. Organizational restructuring efforts in which individuals are laid off from their jobs.

___ 8. Part-time, temporary, or freelance employees.

___ 9. Increasing the decision-making discretion of workers.

___ 10. Dynamic systems that interact with and respond to their environment.

___ 11. The breakdown of jobs into narrow, repetitive tasks.

___ 12. A philosophy of management that is driven by customer needs and expectations.

___ 13. A classification scheme for labeling seventeen basic hand motions.

CHAPTER 3

ORGANIZATIONAL CULTURE AND ENVIRONMENT: THE CONSTRAINTS

Chapter Objectives

1. Differentiate the symbolic from the omnipotent view of management.

2. Define organizational culture.

3. Identify the ten characteristics that make up an organization's culture.

4. Explain how culture constrains managers.

5. Distinguish between the general and specific environment.

6. contrast certain and uncertain environments.

7. Describe the various components in the specific environment.

8. Describe the factors in the general environment.

9. Explain how the environment constrains managers.

Chapter Outline

I. The Manager: Omnipotent or Symbolic?

    A. The Omnipotent View

    B. The Symbolic View

    C. A Synthesis

II. The Organization's Culture

    A. What is Organizational Culture?

        1. Characteristics of an organization's culture

    B. The Source of Culture

    C. Strong Versus Weak Cultures

    D. Influence on Management Practice

III. The Environment

    A. Defining the Environment

        1. General versus specific environment

    B. Assessing Environmental Uncertainty

        1. Degree of change

        2. Degree of complexity

        3. The Organization and its environment

    C. The Specific Environment

        1. Suppliers

        2. Customers

        3. Competitors

        4. Government

        5. Pressure groups

    D. The General Environment

        1. Economic conditions

        2. Political conditions

        3. Social conditions

        4. Global

        5. Technological conditions

    E. Influence on Management Practice

Key Terms

Omnipotent view of Management - The view that managers are directly responsible for an organization's success or failure.

Symbolic view of management - The view that management has only a limited effect on substantive organizational outcomes because of the large number of factors outside of management's control.

Organizational culture - A system of shared meaning within an organization that determines, in large degree, how employs act.

Strong cultures - Organizations in which the key values are intensely held and widely shared.

Environment - Outside institutions or forces that potentially affect an organization's performance.

    General environment - Everything outside the outside the organization.

    Specific environment - The part of the environment that is directly relevant to the achievement of an organization's goals.

Environmental uncertainty - The degree of change and complexity in an organization's environment.

Environmental complexity - The number of components in an organization's environment and the extent of an organization's knowledge about its environmental components.

MULTIPLE CHOICE QUESTIONS

1. Which is true for the omnipotent view of a manager?

    a. A manager only has a limited effect on organization outcomes.
    b. Managers are directly responsible for the success or failure of an organization.
    c. Results of organization actions are influenced by many factors outside the control of management.
    d. The manager's role is to create the illusion of control for the benefit of stockholders, customers, employees, and the public.

2. Which is the most realistic view of a manager?

   a. omnipotent view.
   b. symbolic view.
   c. combination of omnipotent and symbolic view.
   d. none of the above.

3. Which is not true for organization culture?

   a. Culture cannot be analyzed.
   b. Culture is the personality of the company.
   c. Culture governs how managers behave.
   d. Culture is based on perceptions.

4. An organization culture

   a. changes routinely.
   b. is relatively enduring over time.
   c. changes when new workers come into the organization.
   d. never changes.

5. Which is true for a strong corporate culture?

   a. Key values are intensely held and widely shared.
   b. Key values have little influence on employees.
   c. It is unclear what is important and what is not important to workers.
   d. Culture is not likely to constrain managers.

6. The term that best describes the part of the environment that is directly relevant to achievement of organization goals is

   a. environment.
   b. general environment.
   c. specific environment.
   d. environmental uncertainty.

7. If components in the environment change frequently, the environment is said to be

   a. stable.
   b. dynamic.
   c. simple.
   d. complex.

8. If there are few components in the environment and the manager understands these components, the environment is said to be

    a. stable.
    b. dynamic.
    c. simple.
    d. complex.

9. This type of environment occurs when there are few new competitors, few new technological breakthroughs, and little activity by pressure groups.

    a. stable.
    b. dynamic.
    c. simple.
    d. complex.

10. If an organization signs an agreement to produce items for a large department store and this lessens the number of buyers, there is

    a. a decrease in complexity.
    b. an increase in complexity.
    c. a decrease in stability.
    d. an increase in uncertainty.

11. If an organization has to begin dealing with more external factors and more change in these factors, there is

    a. a decrease in complexity.
    b. an increase in complexity.
    c. a decrease in stability.
    d. an increase in uncertainty.

12. Suppliers include

    a. materials and equipment needed to produce the product.
    b. government, customers, and competitors.
    c. materials, equipment, financial resources suppliers, and labor suppliers.
    d. none of the above.

13. The specific environment includes

    a. suppliers, customers, competitors, government, and pressure groups
    b. suppliers, competitors, and technology.
    c. customers, suppliers, society, and pressure groups.
    d. government, pressure groups, the economy, and suppliers.

14. Which is true for the general environment?

    a. The general environment does not have as large an impact on company actions as the specific environment.
    b. The general environment has more impact on company actions than the specific environment.
    c. The general environment has about the same impact on company actions as the specific environment.
    d. The general environment does not affect the company's actions.

15. Political conditions include

    a. general stability the country.
    b. specific attitudes that elected government officials hold toward the role of business in society.
    c. general stability of the country and specific attitudes that elected government officials hold toward the role of business in society.
    d. none of the above.

16. Social conditions include

    a. consumer customs.
    b. consumer tastes.
    c. consumer values.
    d. all of the above.

17. What is the influencing environmental factor when interest rates increase and firms find it difficult to borrow funds?

    a. economic factor.
    b. technological factor.
    c. social factor.
    d. competitive factor.

18. What is the influencing environmental factor when new substitutes are developed by other companies?

    a. economic factor.
    b. technological factor.
    c. social factor.
    d. competitive factor.

19. What is the influencing environmental factor when ideas are developed for improving production machinery?

    a. economic factor.
    b. technological factor.
    c. social factor.
    d. competitive factor.

20. What is the influencing environmental factor when the aging population requires that a company change its product?

    a. economic factor.
    b. technological factor.
    c. social factor.
    d. competitive factor.

TRUE/FALSE QUESTIONS

1. T F   The symbolic view of the manager is that an organization's outcomes are influenced by a number of factors outside the control of management.

2. T F   Internal constraints exist within every organization that restrict a manager's decision options.

3. T F   External constraints come from the organization culture.

4. T F   Because of all the constraints, managers are not very powerful.

5. T F   The personality of the organization is the organization culture.

6. T F   Organization culture is relatively enduring over time and relatively static in its propensity to change.

7. T F   An organization culture is particularly relevant to managers because it establishes constraints upon what they can and cannot do.

8. T F   The organization culture is usually written down in the formal policies of the organization.

9. T F   The general environment includes suppliers, customers, and competitors.

10. T F   The specific environment is unique to each organization and changes as the organization changes.

11. T F   Environmental uncertainty refers to the amount of change and complexity in the organization environment.

12. T F   An organization that deals with fewer customers, suppliers, competitors, and government agencies has more uncertainty in its external environment than a company that deals with more customers, suppliers, competitors, and government agencies.

13. T F   Managers want to minimize the amount of uncertainty in the environment because it threatens organization effectiveness.

14. T F   Government regulation limits the choices available to managers.

15. T F   A manager does not need to adapt her/his practices to social conditions in the environment.

MATCH TERMS WITH DEFINITIONS

a. Organizational culture
b. Symbolic view of management
c. Environmental uncertainty
d. Omnipotent view of management
e. Environmental complexity
f. Environment
g. Specific environment
h. General environment

___ 1. The view that managers are directly responsible for an organization's success or failure.

___ 2. Outside institutions or forces that potentially affect an organization's performance.

___ 3. The degree of change and complexity in an organization's environment.

___ 4. The number of components in an organization's environment and the extent of an organization's knowledge about its environmental components.

___ 5. Everything outside the outside the organization.

___ 6. The part of the environment that is directly relevant to the achievement of an organization's goals.

___ 7. The view that management has only a limited effect on substantive organizational outcomes because of the large number of factors outside of management's control.

___ 8. A system of shared meaning within an organization that determines, in large degree, how employs act.

CHAPTER 4

MANAGING IN A GLOBAL ENVIRONMENT

Chapter Objectives

1. Explain the importance of viewing management from a global perspective.

2. Describe problems created by national parochialism.

3. Contrast multinational and transnational corporations.

4. Explain why many countries have become part of regional trading alliances.

5. Describe the typical stages by which organizations go international.

6. Explain the four dimensions of national culture.

7. Describe US culture according to the four dimensions.

8. Describe the challenges of being a manager on global assignment.

Chapter Outline

I. Who Owns What?

II. Overcoming Parochialism

III. The Changing Global Environment

    A. From Multinationals to Transnationals to Borderless Organizations

    B. Regional Trading Alliances

        1. The European Union

        2. North American Free Trade Agreement (NAFTA)

        3. What's next? a Pacific-Rim Bloc?

        4. Eastern Europe and Capitalism

IV. How Organizations Go International

V. Managing in a Foreign Environment

    A. The Legal-Political Environment

    B. The Economic Environment

    C. The Cultural Environment

        1. Individualism versus Collectivism

        2. Power Distance

        3. Uncertainty Avoidance

        4. Quantity versus Quality of Life

        5. A Guide for United States Managers

VI. Is a Global Assignment for You?

Key Terms

Parochialism - A selfish, narrow view of the world; an inability to recognize differences between people.

Multinational Corporation (MNC) - Companies that maintain significant operations in more than one country simultaneously but manage them all from one base in a home country.

Transnational Corporation (TNC) - A company that maintains significant operations in more than one country simultaneously and decentralizes decision making in each operation to the local country.

European Union (EU) - A union of fifteen European nations created to eliminate national barriers to travel, employment, investment, and trade.

National Culture - The attitudes and perspectives shared by individuals from a specific country that shape their behaviors and the way they see the world.

    Individualism - A cultural dimension in which people are supposed to look after their own interests and those of their immediate family.

    Collectivism - A cultural dimension in which people expect others in their group to look after them and protect them when they are in trouble.

Power Distance - A cultural measure of the extent to which a society accepts the unequal distribution of power in institutions and organizations.

Uncertainty Avoidance - A cultural measure of the degree to which people tolerate risk and unconventional behavior.

Quantity of Life - A national culture attribute describing the extent to which societal values are characterized by assertiveness and materialism.

Quality of Life - A national culture attribute that reflects the emphasis placed on relationships and concern for others.

Organizational Socialization - The process that employees go through to adapt to an organization's culture.

Culture Shock - The feelings of confusion, disorientation, and emotional upheaval caused by being immersed in a new culture.

MULTIPLE CHOICE QUESTIONS

1. Which is true for multinational corporations?

   a. A MNC has significant operations in more than one country.
   b. The concept of MNC has been around for centuries.
   c. A MNC focuses on developing specific, different strategies and products.
   d. A MNC is a large corporation.

2. An example of regional cooperation in global competition is

   a. European Union.
   b. U.S. and Canadian Alliance.
   c. U.S. and Mexico Border Zones.
   d. all of the above.

3. The nations united in 1992 to become a single market are called

   a. European Union.
   b. U.S. and Canadian Alliance.
   c. U.S. and Mexico Border Zones.
   d. U.S. and Mexico Free Trade.

4. The legal-political environment is an important consideration foreign environments because

   a. all foreign environments are unstable.
   b. laws are similar in foreign nations, but different from the U.S.
   c. differences in U.S. and foreign operations require that managers understand constraints under which they operate in foreign nations.
   d. none of the above.

5. Economic concerns are important for corporations that operate in the international environment because they can be affected by

   a. fluctuating exchange rates.
   b. fluctuating value of the foreign investment.
   c. diverse tax policies.
   d. all of the above.

6. Which is not true for the cultural environment?

   a. The cultural environment is fairly straightforward.
   b. Often "natives" are not capable of explaining unique characteristics of their culture to outsiders.
   c. The national culture has a greater effect on employees than does their organizational culture.
   d. Obtaining information about a country's culture is more difficult than obtaining economic and legal information.

7. People in the U.S. have the following culture characteristics:

   a. informal, competitive, individualistic, high power distance.
   b. value for punctuality, value for cleanliness, individualistic, and competitive.
   c. informal, noncompetitive, and direct.
   d. none of the above.

8. The measure of degree to which people tolerate risk and unconventional behavior.

   a. individualism.
   b. collectivism.
   c. power distance.
   d. uncertainty avoidance.

9. People expect others to look out after them.

   a. individualism.
   b. collectivism.
   c. power distance.
   d. uncertainty avoidance.

10. The extent to which a society accepts the unequal distribution of power in an organization.

    a. individualism.
    b. collectivism.
    c. power distance.
    d. uncertainty avoidance.

11. An employee who shows a great deal of respect for those in authority is

    a. low in power distance.
    b. low in uncertainty avoidance.
    c. high in power distance.
    d. high in uncertainty avoidance.

12. Stress and aggressiveness of workers because of ambiguity in the society illustrates

    a. low power distance.
    b. low uncertainty avoidance.
    c. high power distance.
    d. high uncertainty avoidance.

13. Low job mobility and lifetime employment policies, formal rules, little tolerance for unconventional behavior and ideas illustrates

    a. low power distance.
    b. low uncertainty avoidance.
    c. high power distance.
    d. high uncertainty avoidance.

14. The inequities between managers and workers is played down; workers are not in awe of the boss illustrates

    a. low power distance.
    b. low uncertainty avoidance.
    c. high power distance.
    d. high uncertainty avoidance.

15. In this stage of evolution into a global organization, a company might contract with a foreign manufacturer to produce products for sale in that country.

    a. established international operations.
    b. passive response.
    c. transnational operations.
    d. initial overt entry.

16. Jason Neal was recently sent to Peru as a manager for his U.S. based company. Jason only spoke English and had not traveled outside the country before this assignment. He complained to his regional manager that his Peruvian counterparts were very rude because they insisted on standing too close during conversations. He could be described as

    a. culturally sensitive.
    b. parochial.
    c. a complainer.
    d. appreciating foreign values.

17. Transnational companies

    a. replicate domestic success in other countries.
    b. are identical to multinationals.
    c. make decisions in the home country office and distribute them to local units.
    d. place decision making in the local operation offices.

18. "American" cars are

    a. made in the U.S. by U.S. firms.
    b. made in the U.S. by Japanese firms.
    c. made in Canada by U.S. firms.
    d. all of the above.

19. What is the largest economic market in the world based on gross domestic product in 1992?

    a. Japan.
    b. United States.
    c. Europe.
    d. China.

20. To be a successful international manager, an individual needs

    a. a positive outlook.
    b. relationship skills.
    c. perceptual skills.
    d. all of the above.

TRUE/FALSE QUESTIONS

1. T F   People with a parochial perspective recognize that people in other countries have different ways of living and working.

2. T F   Successful global management requires enhanced sensitivity to differences in national customs and practices.

3. T F   Since international businesses have been around for centuries, multinational corporations are not a recent phenomenon.

4. T F   Diverse political systems, laws, and customs faced by managers of multinational corporations provide both problems and opportunities.

5. T F   A TNC maintains operations in more than one country, but manages them from one base in a home country.

6. T F   Research indicates that the national culture has a greater effect on employees than does their organization culture.

7. T F   A framework to help managers better understand differences in national cultures was developed by Geert Hofstede.

8. T F   Collectivism is a concern of power distance in evaluating national cultures.

9. T F   Individualism refers to a tight social framework in which people expect others in the groups to which they belong to look after them and protect them when they are in trouble.

10. T F   Power distance is a measure of the degree to which people tolerate risk and unconventional behavior.

11. T F   A high power distance society accepts wide differences in power in organizations.

12. T F   In societies that have low uncertainty avoidance, people feel relatively secure.

13. T F   In terms of quality and quantity of life, Hofstede found that the U.S. has the highest quantity of life rating.

14. T F   The U.S. is strongly individualistic, but low on power distance.

15. T F   Regional trading alliances create more powerful economic entities.

MATCH TERMS WITH DEFINITIONS

a.   Multinational Corporation (MNC)
b.   Quantity of Life
c.   Transnational Corporation (TNC)
d.   European Union

e. National Culture
f. Individualism
g. Power Distance
h. Organizational Socialization
i. Culture Shock
j. Collectivism
k. Parochialism
l. Uncertainty Avoidance
m. Quality of Life

___ 1. A cultural dimension in which people are supposed to look after their own interests and those of their immediate family.

___ 2. A company that maintains significant operations in more than one country simultaneously and decentralizes decision making in each operation to the local country.

___ 3. A cultural dimension in which people expect others in their group to look after them and protect them when they are in trouble.

___ 4. A national culture attribute that reflects the emphasis placed on relationships and concern for others.

___ 5. A union of fifteen European nations created to eliminate national barriers to travel, employment, investment, and trade.

___ 6. A cultural measure of the extent to which a society accepts the unequal distribution of power in institutions and organizations.

___ 7. A cultural measure of the degree to which people tolerate risk and unconventional behavior.

___ 8. A national culture attribute describing the extent to which societal values are characterized by assertiveness and materialism.

___ 9. Companies that maintain significant operations in more than one country simultaneously but manage them all from one base in a home country.

___ 10. The process that employees go through to adapt to an organization's culture.

___ 11. A selfish, narrow view of the world; an inability to recognize differences between people.

___ 12. The feelings of confusion, disorientation, and emotional upheaval caused by being immersed in a new culture.

___ 13. The attitudes and perspectives shared by individuals from a specific country that shape their behaviors and the way they see the world.

CHAPTER 5

SOCIAL RESPONSIBILITY AND MANAGERIAL ETHICS

<u>Chapter Objectives</u>

1. Explain the classical and socioeconomic views of social responsibility.

2. List the arguments for and against business being socially responsible.

3. Differentiate between social responsibility and social responsiveness.

4. Explain the relationship between corporate social responsibility and economic performance.

5. Define stakeholders, and describe their role in social responsibility.

6. Describe values-based management and how it relates to organizational culture.

7. Define ethics.

8. Differentiate four views of ethics.

9. Identify the factors that affect ethical behavior.

10. Describe the stages of moral development.

11. Discuss various ways organizations can improve the ethical behavior of their employees.

<u>Chapter Outline</u>

I. What is Social Responsibility?

   A. Two Opposing Views

      1. The Classical View

      2. The Socioeconomic View

   B. Arguments For and Against Social Responsibility

    C. From Obligations to Responsiveness

II. Social Responsibility and Economic Performance

III. Is Social Responsibility Just Profit-Maximizing Behavior?

IV. Values-Based Management

    A. Purposes of Shared Values

    B. Developing Shared Values

V. A Guide Through the Maze

VI. Managerial Ethics

    A. Four Different Views of Ethics

    B. Factors Affecting Managerial Ethics

        1. Stage of Moral Development

        2. Individual Characteristics

        3. Structural Variables

        4. Organization's Culture

        5. Issue Intensity

    C. Ethics in an International Context

    D. Toward Improving Ethical Behavior

        1. Selection

        2. Codes of Ethics and Decision Rules

        3. Top Management's Leadership

        4. Job Goals

        5. Ethics Training

        6. Comprehensive Performance Appraisal

        7. Independent Social Audits

        8. Formal Protective Mechanisms

Key Terms

Classical View - The view that management's only social responsibility is to maximize profits.

Socioeconomic View - The view that management's social responsibility goes well beyond the making of profits to include protecting and improving society's welfare.

Social Responsibility - An obligation, beyond that required by the law and economics, for a firm to pursue long-term goals that are good for society.

Social Obligation - The obligation of a business to meet its economic and legal responsibilities.

Social Responsiveness - The capacity of a firm to adapt to changing societal conditions.

Cause-related Marketing - Performing social actions that are motivated directly by profits.

Values-based Management - An approach to managing in which managers establish, promote, and practice an organization's shared values.

Stakeholders - Any constituency in the environment that is affected by an organization's decisions and policies.

Ethics - Rules and principles that define right and wrong conduct.

>**Utilitarian View of Ethics** - Decisions are made solely on the basis of their outcomes or consequences.
>
>**Rights View of Ethics** - Decisions are concerned with respecting and protecting basic rights of individuals.
>
>**Theory of Justice View of Ethics** - Decision makers seek to impose and enforce rules fairly and impartially.
>
>**Integrative Social Contracts Theory** - A view that proposes decisions should be made based on empirical (what is) and normative (what should be) factors.

Values - Basic convictions about what is right and wrong.

Ego Strength - A personality characteristic that measures the strength of a person's convictions.

Locus of Control - A personality attribute that measures the degree to which people believe they are masters of their own fate.

Code of Ethics - A formal statement of an organization's primary values and the ethical rules it expects its employees to follow.

MULTIPLE CHOICE QUESTIONS

1. When corporations believe they have a social responsibility to the larger society that creates and sustains them, they are reflecting

    a. the classical view.
    b. the socioeconomic view.
    c. cause-related marketing.
    d. issue intensity.

2. Hiring lobbyists and providing financial support for Political Action Committees in order to minimize surprises and enforce social policies that benefit the firm, is an example of

    a. the classical view.
    b. the socioeconomic view.
    c. cause-related marketing.
    d. issue intensity.

3. The belief that the primary interest of managers should be protecting the interests of their stockholders by maximizing profits is an example of

    a. the classical view.
    b. the socioeconomic view.
    c. cause-related marketing.
    d. issue intensity.

4. An example of an argument for social responsibility related to financial security in the long term is

    a. public expectations.
    b. better environment.
    c. costs.
    d. profits.

5. Those who argue against social responsibility because of costs would suggest that

    a. social responsibility costs are passed on to the customer.
    b. cost are lower with social responsibility.
    c. profits are higher with social responsibility.
    d. all of the above.

6. A company improving air pollution standards at their firm to meet the minimum levels required by law is practicing

   a. social responsibility.
   b. social obligation.
   c. social responsiveness.
   d. issue intensity.

7. A company which voluntarily recalls a toy when it is discovered to be unsafe is practicing

   a. social responsibility.
   b. social obligation.
   c. social responsiveness.
   d. issue intensity.

8. A car company improves their engines so that their cars get higher than the legally required minimum standard for miles per gallon is practicing

   a. social responsibility.
   b. social obligation.
   c. social responsiveness.
   d. issue intensity.

9. Closing a plant that puts 500 people out of work versus closing a plant that puts 50 people our of work illustrates the _____ characteristic of issue intensity.

   a. immediacy of consequences
   b. proximity to the victim
   c. probability of harm
   d. greatness of harm

10. Reducing retirement benefits of current retirees versus reducing retirement benefits of current employees between the ages of 40 and 50 is an example of the _____ characteristic of issue intensity.

    a. immediacy of consequences
    b. proximity to the victim
    c. probability of harm
    d. greatness of harm

11. Layoffs in your own plant versus layoffs you hear about in a far away state illustrates the _____ characteristic of issue intensity.

    a. immediacy of consequences
    b. proximity to the victim
    c. probability of harm
    d. greatness of harm

12. A manager who makes decisions to promote workers based on merit because she believes this is fair to everyone accepts the _____ view on ethics.

    a. utilitarian
    b. rights
    c. theory of justice
    d. code of ethics

13. A manager who sets a policy that allows a worker to challenge the fairness of promotion policies because she wants to make sure that individual's rights are protected subscribes to the _____ view on ethics.

    a. utilitarian
    b. rights
    c. theory of justice
    d. code of ethics

14. A manager who requires all employees to wear safety glasses even though they don't like wearing them because he believes that this policy will make the workplace safer for everyone and will protect the company from a lawsuit believes in the _____ view on ethics.

    a. utilitarian
    b. rights
    c. theory of justice
    d. code of ethics

15. Which is not true for values?

    a. Values are developed from parents, teachers, friends, and others who influence a person.
    b. Values of different managers in the organization are basically the same.
    c. Values are basic convictions about what is right and wrong.
    d. Values are developed in a person's early years.

16. If a company were selling unsafe, high tar cigarettes to third world countries, a manager with high ego strength would be likely to

    a. say he believes that since the cigarettes are unsafe, the company should not sell them, and then he actively campaigns to persuade the company to stop selling the cigarettes.
    b. say he believes that the cigarettes are unsafe and the company should not sell them, but does nothing to encourage the company to stop the practice.
    c. not say what he thinks, but informally suggests that the company stop selling the cigarettes.
    d. not act to change the company practice even if he believes the cigarettes are unsafe.

17. If a company were selling unsafe, high tar cigarettes to third world countries, a manager with an external locus of control would be likely to

   a. say he believes that since the cigarettes are unsafe, the company should not sell them, and then he actively campaigns to persuade the company to stop selling the cigarettes.
   b. say he believes that the cigarettes are unsafe and the company should not sell them, but does nothing to encourage the company to stop the practice.
   c. not say what he thinks, but informally suggests that the company stop selling the cigarettes.
   d. not act to change the company practice even if he believes the cigarettes are unsafe.

18. An organization is more likely to shape high standards for ethical behavior if

   a. managers performance is based on "outcomes".
   b. there is much pressure in an organization.
   c. objectives and performance goals are unclear.
   d. the culture is high in risk tolerance and high in conflict tolerance.

19. Top managers are role models in both word and action because they

   a. imply that their behavior is acceptable for others.
   b. can punish behavior.
   c. can reward behavior with promotions.
   d. all of the above.

20. To create a good corporate values statement, a company should

   a. involve only management.
   b. include every possibility even if trivial.
   c. make sure all departments accept identical values.
   d. leave out religious references.

TRUE/FALSE QUESTIONS

1. T F   The classical view of social responsibility states that a manager's social responsibility goes beyond making a profit.

2. T F   The most outspoken advocate of the classical view of social responsibility is Milton Friedman.

3. T F   Supporters of the socioeconomic view contend that managers must accept social obligations and the costs that go with them so that profits can be maximized in the long-term.

4. T F   Social obligation is the capacity of a firm to respond to social pressures.

5. T F   Social responsibility does not require business to determine what is right or wrong, but business is guided only by social norms.

6. T F   When a company follows pollution control standards because they have been established by the federal government, the company is being socially responsible.

7. T F   At the conventional level of moral development, individuals make decisions based on moral principles.

8. T F   At the preconventional level of moral development, individuals make decisions based on their own personal consequences.

9. T F   The focus of the recent efforts by colleges to raise students' ethical awareness and standards is an attempt to move students to the principled level of moral decision making.

10. T F   The characteristics of the ethical issue itself affects a manager's ethical behavior.

11. T F   When both concentration of effect and immediacy of consequences are high, ethical intensity is reduced.

12. T F   According to the rights view of ethics, decisions are made on the basis of outcomes or consequences.

13. T F   Values are basic convictions about right and wrong that are developed in the early years of life.

14. T F   A culture that is likely to shape high ethical standards is one that is low in risk tolerance and low in conflict tolerance.

15. T F   Codes of ethics should be clearly written so that ethical options are specifically identified.

MATCH TERMS WITH DEFINITIONS

a. Ethics
b. Values
c. Ego Strength
d. Locus of Control
e. Social Responsibility
f. Classical View

g. Code of Ethics
h. Social Obligation
i. Socioeconomic View
j. Cause-related Marketing
k. Social Responsiveness
l. Values-based Management
m. Integrative Social Contracts Theory
n. Rights View of Ethics
o. Stakeholders
p. Theory of Justice View of Ethics
q. Utilitarian View of Ethics

___ 1. The view that management's only social responsibility is to maximize profits.

___ 2. An obligation, beyond that required by the law and economics, for a firm to pursue long-term goals that are good for society.

___ 3. The obligation of a business to meet its economic and legal responsibilities.

___ 4. Performing social actions that are motivated directly by profits.

___ 5. An approach to managing in which managers establish, promote, and practice an organization's shared values.

___ 6. A formal statement of an organization's primary values and the ethical rules it expects its employees to follow.

___ 7. The capacity of a firm to adapt to changing societal conditions.

___ 8. Decisions are concerned with respecting and protecting basic rights of individuals.

___ 9. The view that management's social responsibility goes well beyond the making of profits to include protecting and improving society's welfare.

___ 10. Any constituency in the environment that is affected by an organization's decisions and policies.

___ 11. Decision makers seek to impose and enforce rules fairly and impartially.

___ 12. Basic convictions about what is right and wrong.

___ 13. Rules and principles that define right and wrong conduct.

___ 14. A personality characteristic that measures the strength of a person's convictions.

___ 15. Decisions are made solely on the basis of their outcomes or consequences.

___ 16. A personality attribute that measures the degree to which people believe they are masters of their own fate.

___ 17. A view that proposes decisions should be made based on empirical (what is) and normative (what should be) factors.

CHAPTER 6

DECISION MAKING: THE ESSENCE OF THE MANAGER'S JOB

Chapter Objectives

1. Outline the steps in the decision-making process.

2. Describe the rational decision maker.

3. Explain the limits to rationality.

4. Describe the perfectly rational decision-making process.

5. Describe the boundedly rational decision-making process.

6. Identify the two types of decision problems and the two types of decisions that are used to solve them.

7. Describe the different decision-making styles.

8. Differentiate the decision conditions of certainty, risk, and uncertainty.

9. Identify the advantages and disadvantages of group decisions.

10. Describe four techniques for improving group decision-making.

Chapter Outline

I. The Decision-Making Process

   A. Steps in the Process

      1. Step 1: Identifying a Problem

      2. Step 2: Identifying Decision Criteria

      3. Step 3: Allocating Weights to the Criteria

      4. Step 4: Developing Alternatives

5. Step 5: Analyzing Alternatives

6. Step 6: Selecting an Alternative

7. Step 7: Implementing the Alternative

8. Step 8: Evaluating Decision Effectiveness

II. The Pervasiveness of Decision-Making

III. The Rational Decision-Maker

    A. Assumptions of Rationality

        1. Problem clarity

        2. Goal orientation

        3. Known options

        4. Clear preferences

        5. Constant preferences

        6. No time or cost constraints

        7. Maximum payoff

    B. Limits to Rationality

    C. Bounded Rationality

IV. Problems and Decisions: A Contingency Approach

    A. Types of Problems

        1. Well-structured

        2. Ill-structured

    B. Types of Decisions

        1. Programmed Decisions

        2. Nonprogrammed Decisions

    C. Integration

V. Decision-making Styles

VI. Analyzing Decision Alternatives

    A. Certainty

    B. Risk

    C. Uncertainty

VIII. Group Decision-Making

    A. Advantages and Disadvantages

    B. Effectiveness and Efficiency

    C. Techniques for Improving Group Decision-Making

        1. Brainstorming

        2. Nominal Group Technique

        3. Delphi Technique

        4. Electronic Meetings

Key Terms

Decision-making process - A set of eight steps that include identifying a problem, selecting an alternative, and evaluating the decision's effectiveness.

Problem - A discrepancy between an existing and a desired state of affairs.

Decision criteria - Criteria that define what is relevant in a decision.

Implementation - Conveying a decision to those affected and getting their commitment to it.

Rational - Describe choices that are consistent and value maximizing within specified constraints.

Escalation of commitment - An increased commitment to a previous decision despite evidence that it may have been wrong.

Bounded rationality - Behavior that is rational within the parameters of a simplified model that captures the essential features of a problem.

Satisficing - Acceptance of solutions that are "good enough".

Problem structure

> **Well-structured problems** - Straightforward, familiar, easily defined problems.
>
> **Ill-structured problems** - New problems in which information is ambiguous or incomplete.

Programmed decision - A repetitive decision that can be handled by a routine approach.

Procedure - A series of interrelated sequential steps that can be used to respond to a structured problem.

Rule - An explicit statement that tells managers what they ought or ought not to do.

Policy - A guide that establishes parameters for making decisions.

Nonprogrammed decision - Unique decisions that require a custom-made solution.

Approaches to Problems

> **Problem avoider** - An approach to problems in which the person avoids or ignores information that points to a problem.
>
> **Problem solver** - An approach to problems in which the person tries to solve problems as they come up.,
>
> **Problem seeker** - An approach to problems in which the person actively seeks out problems to solve or new opportunities to pursue.

Decision-making styles

> **Directive style** - A decision-making style characterized by a low tolerance for ambiguity and a rational way of thinking.
>
> **Analytic style** - A decision-making style characterized by a high tolerance for ambiguity and a rational way of thinking.
>
> **Conceptual style** - A decision-making style characterized by a high tolerance for ambiguity and an intuitive way of thinking.
>
> **Behavioral style** - A decision-making style characterized by a low tolerance for ambiguity and an intuitive way of thinking.

Certainty - A situation in which a manager can make accurate decisions because the outcome of every alternative is known.

Risk - Those conditions in which the decision-maker is able to estimate the likelihood of certain outcomes.

Uncertainty - A situation in which a decision-maker has neither certainty nor reasonable estimates available.

Groupthink - The withholding by group members of different views in order to appear in agreement.

Brainstorming - An idea-generating process that encourages alternatives while withholding criticism.

Storyboarding - A variation of brainstorming in which participants identify major issues and brainstorm each of them in order to put together a complete "story" of the total problem.

Lotus blossom technique - Another variation of brainstorming in which a core thought is used as the basis for expanding ideas into an ever-widening series of surrounding ideas (like the petals of a lotus blossom).

Nominal group technique - A decision-making technique in which group members are physically present but operate independently.

Delphi technique - A group decision-making technique in which members never meet face to face.

Electronic meeting - Decision-making groups that interact by way of linked computers.

MULTIPLE CHOICE QUESTIONS

1. The control mechanism in the decision-making process is

    a. allocating weights to the criteria.
    b. developing alternatives.
    c. evaluating decision effectiveness.
    d. analyzing alternatives.

2. A manager who determines that cost, speed, and enlarging capability are relevant to his decision to purchase a new photocopy machine is an example of the _____ phase of the decision-making process.

    a. allocating weights to the criteria
    b. identifying decision criteria
    c. developing alternatives
    d. formulating a problem

3. A perfectly rational decision-maker would

   a. be fully objective and logical.
   b. select the alternative that maximizes a specific goal.
   c. define a problem carefully.
   d. follow all of the above.

4. Escalation of commitment is

   a. usually effective.
   b. a contingency approach in decision-making.
   c. a limit to rationality in decision-making.
   d. profit maximizing.

5. Decision-makers tend to

   a. intermix solutions with problems.
   b. make perfectly rational decisions.
   c. select information for its quality rather than its accessibility.
   d. wait until the end of the decision process to commit to a decision.

6. Bounded rationality is

   a. conveying a decision to those affected and getting their commitment to it.
   b. the withholding by group members of different views in order to appear in agreement.
   c. behavior that is rational within the parameters of a simplified model that captures the essential features of a problem.
   d. an explicit statement that tells managers what they ought or ought not to do.

7. Decisions that are routine are called

   a. nonprogrammed decisions.
   b. programmed decisions.
   c. ill-structured problems.
   d. well-structured problems.

8. The manager of a retail clothing store just found out that some "name brand" merchandise was actually brought into the US illegally. This is an example of

   a. a well-structured problem.
   b. satisficing.
   c. an ill-structured problem.
   d. a programmed decision.

9. Policies, procedures, and rules are developed to help managers deal with

   a. well-structured problems.
   b. groupthink.
   c. bounded rationality.
   d. nonprogrammed decisions.

10. Which of the following is the procedure for snack breaks in a production company?

    a. Each production worker is entitled to a snack break in the morning and in the afternoon each work day.
    b. No food is to be taken into the work area. All snacks must be eaten in the break room.
    c. Employees will be given a morning break beginning at 10AM for production line one and continuing at fifteen minute intervals until all four production lines have taken a break. Workers should report to the production line after a fifteen minute break.
    d. All statements above are procedures.

11. Which of the following is a rule for snack breaks in a production company?

    a. Each production worker is entitled to a snack break in the morning and in the afternoon each work day.
    b. No food is to be taken into the work area. All snacks must be eaten in the break room.
    c. Employees will be given a morning break beginning at 10AM for production line one and continuing at fifteen minute intervals until all four production lines have taken a break. Workers should report to the production line after a fifteen minute break.
    d. All statements above are rules.

12. Which of the following is a policy for snack breaks in a production company?

    a. Each production worker is entitled to a snack break in the morning and in the afternoon each work day.
    b. No food is to be taken into the work area. All snacks must be eaten in the break room.
    c. Employees will be given a morning break beginning at 10AM for production line one and continuing at fifteen minute intervals until all four production lines have taken a break. Workers should report to the production line after a fifteen minute break.
    d. All statements above are policies

13. As a worker moves to higher levels in the organization, she/he is more likely to encounter

    a. ill-structured problems.
    b. nonprogrammed decisions.
    c. nonroutine decisions.
    d. all of the above types of decisions.

14. Mary can repair a saw at quality Production, Inc. in two hours while it takes Mike five hours to make repairs. Assuming that both workers are present, the manager will always choose Mary to make repairs to the saws. This is a decision under

    a. conditions of certainty.
    b. conditions of risk.
    c. conditions of uncertainty.
    d. none of the above.

15. A manager has no idea what alternatives are available for new computer support systems and does not know how she can determine this information. This is a decision under

    a. conditions of certainty.
    b. conditions of risk.
    c. conditions of uncertainty.
    d. none of the above.

16. A manager chooses among three alternatives for advertising (billboards, radio, and newspapers) based on research indicating success in sales for the three alternatives. This is a decision under

    a. conditions of certainty.
    b. conditions of risk.
    c. conditions of uncertainty.
    d. none of the above.

17. Disadvantages for group decision-making include

    a. increases acceptance of the solution.
    b. provides more complete information.
    c. pressure to conform.
    d. all of the above.

18. Groupthink

    a. increases effectiveness in decision-making.
    b. generates more alternatives.
    c. means programmed decision-making.
    d. is the withholding by group members of different views in order to appear in agreement.

19. _____ is a group decision-making method in which group members meet face-to-face but operate independently.

   a. Brainstorming
   b. Nominal group technique
   c. Delphi technique
   d. Groupthink

20. An advantage of the Delphi technique is

   a. It insulates group members from the undue influence of others.
   b. It is very efficient since it can be done very quickly.
   c. It is useful in developing a wide range of alternatives.
   d. All of the above are advantages.

TRUE/FALSE QUESTIONS

1. T F The decision-making process is designed for individual decision-making rather than group decision-making.

2. T F A problem is a discrepancy between an existing and desired state of affairs.

3. T F Some discrepancies may not be considered problems because there is no pressure to take action to correct the situation.

4. T F Implementation is merely conveying the decision to those affected.

5. T F Evaluating decision effectiveness is a mechanism for control.

6. T F Evaluating the decision may cause managers to return to an earlier step in the decision process.

7. T F Decision-making is important for only two management functions: planning and leading.

8. T F Decision-making is synonymous with managing.

9. T F Most decisions that managers face do not meet all the tests of rationality.

10. T F Sometimes rationality in decision-making is limited because of prior decisions that have been made by managers.

11. T F Well-structured problems are usually solved with nonprogrammed decisions.

12. T F Lower level managers usually deal with repetitive problems and rely on programmed decisions.

13. T F When the decision-maker knows the probability of occurrences of alternatives, the decision is made under conditions of uncertainty.

14. T F The nominal group technique is a group decision-making method in which members meet face-to-face, but operate independently.

15. T F Groupthink means that group members will feel free to have different views from other group members.

MATCH TERMS WITH DEFINITIONS

a. Certainty
b. Uncertainty
c. Brainstorming
d. Nominal Group technique
e. Risk
f. Groupthink
g. Storyboarding
h. Delphi technique
i. Rational
j. Problem
k. Bounded rationality
l. Policy
m. Procedure
n. Satisficing
o. Rule

___ 1. A discrepancy between an existing and a desired state of affairs.

___ 2. The withholding by group members of different views in order to appear in agreement.

___ 3. Describe choices that are consistent and value maximizing within specified constraints.

___ 4. Those conditions in which the decision-maker is able to estimate the likelihood of certain outcomes.

___ 5. Acceptance of solutions that are "good enough".

___ 6. A variation of brainstorming in which participants identify major issues and brainstorm each of them in order to put together a complete "story" of the total problem.

___ 7. A series of interrelated sequential steps that can be used to respond to a structured problem.

___ 8. A group decision-making technique in which members never meet face to face.

___ 9. A guide that establishes parameters for making decisions.

___ 10. Behavior that is rational within the parameters of a simplified model that captures the essential features of a problem.

___ 11. A situation in which a manager can make accurate decisions because the outcome of every alternative is known.

___ 12. An explicit statement that tells managers what they ought or ought not to do.

___ 13. A situation in which a decision-maker has neither certainty nor reasonable estimates available.

___ 14. An idea-generating process that encourages alternatives while withholding criticism.

___ 15. A decision-making technique in which group members are physically present but operate independently.

CHAPTER 7

FOUNDATIONS OF PLANNING

Chapter Objectives

1. Define planning.

2. Explain the potential benefits of planning.

3. Distinguish between strategic and operational plans.

4. State when directional plans are preferred over specific plans.

5. Differentiate between single-use and strategic plans.

6. Identify three contingency factors in planning.

7. Explain the commitment concept.

8. Explain why an organization's stated objectives might not be its real objectives.

9. Describe a typical MBO program.

10. Explain how MBO uses goals as motivators.

Chapter Outline

I. The Definition of Planning

II. Purposes of Planning

III. Planning and Performance

IV. Myths about Planning

V. Types of Plans

    A. Strategic Versus Operational Plans

    B. Short-Term Versus Long-Term Plans

C. Specific Versus Directional Plans

D. Frequency of Use

VI. Contingency Factors in Planning

A. Level in the Organization

B. Degree of Environmental Uncertainty

C. Length of Future Commitments

VIII. Objectives: The Foundation of Planning

A. Multiplicity of Objectives

B. Real Versus Stated Objectives

C. Traditional Objective Setting

D. Management by Objectives

1. What is MBO?

2. Steps in a Typical MBO Program

3. Does MBO work?

Key Terms

Types of Plans

Strategic Plans - Plans that are organization-wide, establish overall objectives, and position an organization in terms of its environment.

Operational Plans - Plans that specify details on how overall objectives are to be achieved.

Short-term Plans - Plans that cover less than one year.

Long-term Plans - Plans that extend beyond five years.

Specific Plans - Plans that are clearly defined and leave no room for interpretation.

Directional Plans - Flexible plans that set out general guidelines.

57

Single-use Plan - A one-time plan that's specifically designed to meet the needs of a unique situation and is created in response to nonprogrammed decisions that managers make.

Standing Plans - Ongoing plans that provide guidance for activities repeatedly performed in the organization and that are created in response to programmed decisions that managers make.

Commitment Concept - Plans should extend far enough to see through current commitments.

Objectives - Desired outcomes for individuals, groups, or entire organizations.

Stated Objectives - Official statements of what an organization says and what it wants various publics to believe are its objectives.

Real Objectives - Objectives that an organization actually pursues, as defined by the actions of its members.

Traditional Objective Setting - Objectives are set at the top and then broken down into subgoals for each level in an organization. The top imposes its standards on everyone below.

Means-ends Chain - An integrated network of organizational objectives in which higher-level objectives, which serve as the means for their accomplishment.

Management by Objectives (MBO) - A system in which specific performance objectives are jointly determined by subordinates and their superiors, progress toward objectives is periodically reviewed, and rewards are allocated on the basis of this progress.

MULTIPLE CHOICE QUESTIONS

1. The purpose of planning is to

    a. give direction.
    b. reduce the impact of change.
    c. set standards to facilitate control and minimize redundancy.
    d. all of the above.

2. Which is not true for planning?

    a. Planning forces managers to look ahead and anticipate change.
    b. Planning makes coordination of activities more difficult.
    c. Planning includes developing objectives.
    d. Without planning, there is no control.

3. Plans that specify details on how overall objectives are to be achieved are _____ plans.

   a. operational
   b. strategic
   c. specific
   d. directional

4. Flexible plans that set out general guidelines are

   a. operational
   b. strategic
   c. specific
   d. directional

5. _____ plans are organization wide, establish overall objectives, and position an organization in terms of its environment.

   a. operational
   b. strategic
   c. specific
   d. directional

6. _____ plans are clearly defined and leave no room for interpretation.

   a. operational
   b. strategic
   c. specific
   d. directional

7. A _____ plan is an example of a complete, exact plan for training employees.

   a. short-term
   b. specific
   c. operational
   d. long-term

8. A _____ plan is a plan developed to illustrate how a company can increase its market share.

   a. short-term
   b. specific
   c. operational
   d. long-term

9. Operational plans tend to

   a. cover shorter time periods than strategic plans.
   b. include a broader area than strategic plans.
   c. be much less specific than strategic plans.
   d. tend to be long-term plans.

10. A _____ plan is described by its level of Specificity.

    a. operational
    b. directional
    c. short-term
    d. none of the above

11. A _____ plan is described by its Breadth.

    a. operational
    b. directional
    c. short-term
    d. none of the above

12. A contingency factor in planning related to organization stages such as growth and maturity is the

    a. level in the organization.
    b. life cycle in the organization.
    c. degree of environmental uncertainty.
    d. length of future commitments.

13. A contingency factor in planning that effects the manager's role in strategic planning is the

    a. level in the organization.
    b. life cycle in the organization.
    c. degree of environmental uncertainty.
    d. length of future commitments.

14. An example of this contingency factor is that if rapid technological, social, or economic changes occur, well-defined plans will likely hinder an organization's performance.

    a. level in the organization.
    b. life cycle in the organization.
    c. degree of environmental uncertainty.
    d. length of future commitments.

15. Objectives

    a. provide direction for management decisions.
    b. are goals of the organization.
    c. are desired outcomes for individuals, grouped, or entire organizations.
    d. all of the above.

16. An approach to setting objectives from top managers downward through the organization is

    a. real objective.
    b. traditional objective setting.
    c. stated objective.
    d. MBO.

17. An example of _____ is a boss and a worker together decide that the worker will increase his productivity by 8% over the next year. They then meet over that year to assess progress and the worker is rewarded at the fulfillment of the goal.

    a. real objective.
    b. traditional objective setting.
    c. stated objective.
    d. MBO.

18. An example of _____ is an official statement that the university class size will be kept at thirty students.

    a. real objective.
    b. traditional objective setting.
    c. stated objective.
    d. MBO.

19. According to research studies, which contingency variable may explain the instances when MBO fails?

    a. organization constraints that undermine MBO ideology.
    b. unsupportive culture.
    c. lack of top management commitment.
    d. all of the above

20. Which of the following research conclusions is not related MBO?

    a. Feedback on one's performance leads to higher performance.
    b. Hard goals result in a higher level of individual performance than do easy goals.
    c. Participation seems to induce individuals to establish more difficult goals.
    d. Participation decreases one's goal aspiration level.

TRUE/FALSE QUESTIONS

1. T F   Planning is concerned with desired "ends", but not "means".

2. T F   All managers engage in planning, even though for some managers all of their planning is informal.

3. T F   Planning gives direction, reduces the impact of change, minimizes waste, and sets standards to facilitate control.

4. T F   Organizations that formally plan always outperform those that do not formally plan.

5. T F   In those research studies where formal planning has not led to higher performance, the environment is typically the culprit.

6. T F   Strategic plans specify details on how overall objectives are to be achieved.

7. T F   Short-term plans cover less than a year.

8. T F   When uncertainty is high, it is preferable to use directional plans instead of specific plans.

9. T F   As managers rise in the hierarchy, their planning becomes more operational.

10. T F   Managers should rely more heavily on directional plans in an organizations's infancy.

11. T F   Short-term planning is more prevalent than long-term planning in the maturity stage of the organization life cycle.

12. T F   Objectives are goals or desired outcomes.

13. T F   All organizations have multiple objectives.

14. T F   In MBO, objectives are unilaterally set by the boss and assigned to workers.

15. T F   A lack of top management commitment and involvement will quickly undermine any MBO program.

MATCH TERMS WITH DEFINITIONS

a. Traditional Objective Setting
b. MBO
c. Commitment Concept
d. Directional Plans
e. Long-term Plans
f. Short-term Plans
g. Specific Plans
h. Strategic Plans
i. Operational Plans
j. Single-use Plan
k. Standing Plans
l. Objectives
m. Stated Objectives
n. Means-ends Chain
o. Real Objectives

____ 1. Plans should extend far enough to see through current commitments.

____ 2. Plans that cover less than one year.

____ 3. Plans that are clearly defined and leave no room for interpretation.

____ 4. Flexible plans that set out general guidelines.

____ 5. Plans that are organization-wide, establish overall objectives, and position an organization in terms of its environment.

____ 6. A one-time plan that's specifically designed to meet the needs of a unique situation and is created in response to nonprogrammed decisions that managers make.

____ 7. Objectives that an organization actually pursues, as defined by the actions of its members.

____ 8. Ongoing plans that provide guidance for activities repeatedly performed in the organization and that are created in response to programmed decisions that managers make.

____ 9. Plans that extend beyond five years.

____ 10. A system in which specific performance objectives are jointly determined by subordinates and their superiors, progress toward objectives is periodically reviewed, and rewards are allocated on the basis of this progress.

___ 11. An integrated network of organizational objectives in which higher-level objectives, which serve as the means for their accomplishment.

___ 12. Desired outcomes for individuals, groups, or entire organizations.

___ 13. Objectives are set at the top and then broken down into subgoals for each level in an organization. The top imposes its standards on everyone below.

___ 14. Official statements of what an organization says and what it wants various publics to believe are its objectives.

___ 15. Plans that specify details on how overall objectives are to be achieved.

CHAPTER 8

STRATEGIC MANAGEMENT

Chapter Objectives

1. Explain the importance of strategic planning.

2. Differentiate corporate-level, business-level and functional-level strategies.

3. Describe the steps in the strategic management process.

4. Explain SWOT analysis.

5. Differentiate the various grand strategies.

6. Describe the four business groups in the BCG matrix.

7. Identify and contrast the four adaptive business-level strategies.

8. Describe how to assess an organization's competitive advantage.

9. Describe how TQM is used as a strategic weapon.

Chapter Outline

I. The Increasing Importance of Strategic Planning

II. Levels of Strategy

   A. Corporate-Level Strategy

   B. Business-Level Strategy

   C. Functional-Level Strategy

III. The Strategic Management Process

   A. Step 1: Identifying the Organization's Current Mission, Objectives, and Strategies

   B. Step 2: Analyzing the External Environment

C. Step 3: Identifying Opportunities and Threats

D. Step 4: Analyzing the Organization's Resources

E. Step 5: Identifying Strengths and Weaknesses

F. Step 6: Formulating Strategies

G. Step 7: Implementing Strategies

H. Step 8: Evaluating Results

IV. Corporate-Level Strategic Frameworks

A. Grand Strategies

1. Stability Strategy

2. Growth Strategy

3. Retrenchment Strategy

4. Combination

B. Corporate Portfolio Matrix

V. Business-Level Strategic Frameworks

A. Adaptive Strategies

1. Defenders

2. Prospectors

3. Analyzers

4. Reactors

B. Competitive Strategies

1. Industry Analysis

a. Barriers to entry

b. Threat of substitutes

c. Bargaining power of buyers

        d.   Bargaining power of supplier

        e.   Existing rivalry

    2. Selecting a Competitive Advantage

        a.   Cost leadership

        b.   Differentiation

    3. Sustaining a Competitive Advantage

VI. TQM As a Strategic Weapon

Key Terms

Corporate-level strategy - Seeks to determine what businesses a corporation should be in.

Business-level strategy - Seeks to determine how a corporation should compete in each of its businesses.

Strategic business unit (SBU) - A single business or collection of businesses that is independent and formulates its own strategy.

Functional-level strategy - Seeks to determine how to support the business-level strategy.

Strategic management process - A eight-step process encompassing strategic planning, implementation, and evaluation.

Mission - The purpose of an organizations.

SWOT analysis - Analysis of an organizations's strengths and weaknesses, and its environmental opportunities and threats.

    Opportunities - Positive external environmental factors.

    Threats - Negative external environmental factors.

    Strengths - Activities the firm does well or resources it controls.

    Weaknesses - Activities the firm doesn't do well or resources it needs but doesn't have.

Distinctive competence - The exceptional or unique skills and resources that determine the organizations's competitive weapons.

Stability strategy - A corporate-level strategy characterized by an absence of significant change.

Growth strategy - A corporate-level strategy that seeks to increase the level of the organization's operations. this typically includes increasing revenues, employees, and/or market share.

> **Related diversification** - A way that companies choose to grow that involves merging with or acquiring similar firms.
>
> **Merger** - When two or more firms, usually of similar size, combine into one through an exchange of stock.
>
> **Acquisition** - When one company acquires another company through a payment of cash or stock or some combination of the two.
>
> **Unrelated diversification** - A way that companies choose to grow that involves merging with or acquiring unrelated firms, or firms that are not directly related to what the company does.

Retrenchment strategy - A corporate-level strategy that seeks to reduce the size or diversity of an organization's operations.

Combination strategy - A corporate-level strategy that pursues two or more of the following strategies - stability, growth, or retrenchment - simultaneously.

BCG matrix - Strategy tool to guide resource allocation decisions based on market share and growth of SBU's.

> **Cash cows** - Products that demonstrate low growth but have a high market share.
>
> **Stars** - Products that demonstrate high growth and have high market share.
>
> **Question marks** - Products that demonstrate high growth but have low market share.
>
> **Dogs** - Products that demonstrate low growth and have low market share.

Cumulative experience curve - Assumes that when a business increases the amount of product manufactured, the per-unit cost of the product will decrease.

Business-level strategies (Miles and Snow)

> **Defender** - A business-level strategy that seeks stability by producing only a limited set of products directed at a narrow segment of the total potential market.
>
> **Prospector** - A business-level strategy that seeks innovation by finding and exploiting new product and market opportunities.

Analyzer - A business-level strategy that seeks to minimize risk by following competitive innovations only after they have proven successful.

Reactors - A business-level strategy that characterizes inconsistent and unstable decision patterns.

Business-level strategies (Porter)

Cost leadership strategy - The strategy an organization follows when it wants to be the lowest-cost producer in its industry.

Differentiation strategy - The strategy a firm follows when it wants to be unique in its industry along dimensions widely valued by buyers.

Focus strategy - The strategy a company follows when it pursues a cost or differentiation advantage in a narrow industry segment.

Stuck in the middle - Descriptive of organizations that cannot compete through cost leadership, differentiation, or focus strategies.

MULTIPLE CHOICE QUESTIONS

1. Business-level strategy seeks to answer which question?

    a. How do we support the selected strategy?
    b. In what set of businesses should we be involved?
    c. How should we compete in each of our businesses?
    d. None of the above.

2. Which of the following is an example of a functional-level strategy?

    a. plans to integrate operations of three product areas.
    b. plans that pinpoint consumers between the ages of 25 and 35 as the target customer group.
    c. plans that involve the selection of two primary product areas for focus of operations.
    d. plans determining how marketing and production can together to produce a consumer product.

3. Which step in the strategic management process includes developing distinct competencies?

    a. Analyzing the environment
    b. Identifying opportunities and threats
    c. Analyzing organization resources
    d. Identifying strengths and weaknesses

4. Which step in the strategic management process is complete when management has grasped what is taking place in its environment and is aware of trends that might affect operations?

    a. Analyzing the environment
    b. Identifying opportunities and threats
    c. Analyzing organization resources
    d. Identifying strengths and weaknesses

5. For which step in the strategic management process are pending legislation and competitors' activities important considerations?

    a. Analyzing the environment
    b. Identifying opportunities and threats
    c. Analyzing organization resources
    d. Identifying strengths and weaknesses

6. For which step in the strategic management process are determining employee skills and determining the organization's cash position important considerations?

    a. Analyzing the environment
    b. Identifying opportunities and threats
    c. Analyzing organization resources
    d. Identifying strengths and weaknesses

7. Which step in the strategic management process includes developing a list of factors in the external environment that impact the company positively and factors that impact the company negatively?

    a. Analyzing the environment
    b. Identifying opportunities and threats
    c. Analyzing organization resources
    d. Identifying strengths and weaknesses

8. A merger is an example of this corporate-level strategy:

    a. growth
    b. stability
    c. retrenchment
    d. combination

9. Selling off parts of the business is an example of this corporate-level strategy:

   a. growth
   b. stability
   c. retrenchment
   d. combination

10. Which product category in the BCG matrix has high growth and high market share?

    a. cash cow
    b. question mark
    c. star
    d. dog

11. The suggested strategy for products that fit this category of the BCG matrix is to generate funds so that investments can be made in other products:

    a. cash cow
    b. question mark
    c. star
    d. dog

12. A strategy in the adaptive strategy framework that often leads to failure is the _____ strategy.

    a. defender
    b. reactor
    c. prospector
    d. analyzer

13. A strategy in the adaptive strategy framework that is characterized by a loose organization structure is the _____ strategy.

    a. defender
    b. reactor
    c. prospector
    d. analyzer

14. This adaptive strategy involves imitating competitors:

    a. defender
    b. reactor
    c. prospector
    d. analyzer

15. Which of Michael Porter's competitive forces is related to switching costs?

    a. barriers to entry
    b. threats of substitute products
    c. bargaining power of buyers
    d. bargaining power of suppliers

16. Which of Michael Porter's competitive forces is related to buyer loyalty?

    a. barriers to entry
    b. threats of substitute products
    c. bargaining power of buyers
    d. bargaining power of suppliers

17. Which of Porter's strategies is set when companies take advantage of economies of scale?

    a. cost-leadership
    b. focus
    c. differentiation
    d. combination

18. Users of this strategy would emphasize brand image to compare themselves to rivals:

    a. cost-leadership
    b. focus
    c. differentiation
    d. combination

19. An example of this strategy is producing a product for weight conscious people in sufficient numbers to gain economies of scale:

    a. cost-leadership
    b. focus
    c. differentiation
    d. combination

20. How can organizations sustain a competitive advantage?

    a. reducing price to gain volume (if there are strong economies of scale)
    b. creating barriers that make imitation difficult
    c. contracting with suppliers
    d. all of the above

TRUE/FALSE QUESTIONS

1. T F   Strategic planning is a concept that applies only to business organizations.

2. T F   Organizations that are in multiple businesses need to develop different strategies for different organization levels.

3. T F   Corporate-level strategy seeks to answer the question: How should we compete in each of our businesses?

4. T F   The strategic management process and strategic planning are synonymous terms.

5. T F   After analyzing organization resources, the manager needs to develop a list of opportunities and threats.

6. T F   Managers identify strengths and weaknesses to determine where the company can develop distinctive competencies.

7. T F   Organization culture has little impact on strategic planning.

8. T F   The final step in the strategic management process is implementation of the strategy.

9. T F   An approach to corporate-level strategy is called the adaptive strategy framework.

10. T F   A corporate-level strategy that seeks to reduce size or diversity of the organization operations is called retrenchment.

11. T F   The location of a product on the BCG matrix is determined by company market share and anticipated market growth.

12. T F   According to the BCG matrix, cash cows have low market share, but high anticipated market growth.

13. T F   Of the four strategies in the adaptive strategy framework, the prospector strategy often leads to failure.

14. T F   According to Michael Porter, understanding industry competitive factors is not essential in developing strategic alternatives.

15. T F   A focus strategy is a cost-leadership or differentiation strategy that has been developed for a specific market.

MATCHING TERMS WITH DEFINITIONS

a. Stability strategy
b. BCG matrix
c. Unrelated diversification
d. Business-level strategy
e. SWOT analysis
f. Merger
g. Cumulative experience curve
h. Strategic management process
i. Growth strategy
j. Related diversification
k. Strategic business unit (SBU)
l. Retrenchment strategy
m. Distinctive competence
n. Acquisition
o. Corporate-level strategy

___ 1. A corporate-level strategy characterized by an absence of significant change.

___ 2. Seeks to determine how a corporation should compete in each of its businesses.

___ 3. When two or more firms, usually of similar size, combine into one through an exchange of stock.

___ 4. Analysis of an organizations's strengths and weaknesses, and its environmental opportunities and threats.

___ 5. A corporate-level strategy that seeks to reduce the size or diversity of an organization's operations.

___ 6. The exceptional or unique skills and resources that determine the organizations's competitive weapons.

___ 7. When one company acquires another company through a payment of cash or stock or some combination of the two.

___ 8. Seeks to determine what businesses a corporation should be in.

___ 9. A single business or collection of businesses that is independent and formulates its own strategy.

___ 10. A corporate-level strategy that seeks to increase the level of the organization's operations. this typically includes increasing revenues, employees, and/or market share.

___ 11. A way that companies choose to grow that involves merging with or acquiring similar firms.

___ 12. A eight-step process encompassing strategic planning, implementation, and evaluation.

___ 13. Assumes that when a business increases the amount of product manufactured, the per-unit cost of the product will decrease.

___ 14. A way that companies choose to grow that involves merging with or acquiring unrelated firms, or firms that are not directly related to what the company does.

___ 15. Strategy tool to guide resource allocation decisions based on market share and growth of SBU's.

CHAPTER 9

PLANNING TOOLS AND TECHNIQUES

Chapter Objectives

1. Describe techniques for scanning the environment.

2. Contrast quantitative and qualitative forecasting.

3. Explain why budgets are popular.

4. List two approaches to budgeting.

5. Differentiate Gantt charts from load charts.

6. Identify the steps in a PERT network.

7. State the factors that determine a product's breakeven point.

8. Describe the requirements for using linear programming.

9. discuss how simulation can be a planning tool.

10. List five steps toward better time management.

Chapter Outline

I. Techniques for Assessing the Environment

    A. Environmental Scanning

    B. Forecasting

        1. Types of Forecasts

            a. Revenue forecasting

            b. Technological forecasting

        2. Forecasting Techniques

            a. Quantitative forecasting

  b. Qualitative forecasting

 3. Forecasting Effectiveness

 4. Benchmarking for TQM

II. Budgets

 A. Types of Budgets

  1. Revenue Budgets

  2. Expense Budgets

  3. Profit Budgets

  4. Cash Budgets

  5. Capital Expenditure Budgets

  6. Variable Budgets

 B. Approaches to Budgeting

  1. Incremental Budgets

   2. Zero-base Budgets

III. Operational Planning Tools

 A. Scheduling

  1. Gantt Chart

  2. Load Chart

  3. PERT Network Analysis

 B. Breakeven Analysis

 C. Linear Programming

 D. Queuing Theory

 E. Probability Theory

 F. Marginal Analysis

    G. Simulation

IV. Time Management: A Guide to Personal Planning

    A. Time as a Scarce Resource

    B. Focusing on Discretionary Time

    C. How Do You Use Your Time?

    D. Five Steps to Improve Time Management

    E. Some Additional Points to Consider

        1. Follow the 10-90 Principle.

        2. Know Your Productivity Cycle.

        3. Remember Parkinson's Law.

        4. Group less Important Activities Together.

        5. Minimize Disruptions.

        6. Beware of Wasting Time in Poorly Run Meetings.

Key Terms

Environmental scanning - The screening of large amounts of information to detect emerging trends and create scenarios.

Competitor intelligence - Environmental scanning activity that seeks to identify who competitors are, what they're doing, and how their actions will affect the focus organization.

Scenario - A consistent view of what the future is likely to be.

Forecasts - Predictions of future outcomes.

    Revenue forecasting - Predicting future revenues.

    Technological forecasting - Predicting changes in technology and when new technologies are likely to be economically feasible.

Forecasting techniques

> **Quantitative forecasting** - Applies a set of mathematical rules to a series of past data to predict future outcomes.

> **Qualitative forecasting** - Uses the judgment and opinions of knowledgeable individuals to predict future outcomes.

Benchmarking - The search for the best practices among competitors or noncompetitors that lead to their superior performance.

Budget - A numerical plan for allocating resources to specific activities.

> **Revenue budget** - A budget that projects future sales.

> **Expense budget** - A budget that lists the primary activities undertaken by a unit and allocates a dollar amount to each.

> **Profit budget** - A budget used by separate units of an organization that combines revenue and expense budgets to determine the unit's profit contribution.

> **Cash budget** - A budget that forecasts how much cash an organization will have on hand and how much it will need to meet expenses.

> **Capital expenditure budget** - a budget that forecasts investments in property, buildings, and major equipment.

> **Fixed budget** - A budget that assumes a fixed level of sales or production.

> **Variable budget** - A budget that takes into account those costs that vary with volume.

Incremental (or traditional) budget - A budget that allocates funds to departments according to allocations in the previous period

Zero-base budgeting (ZBB) - A system in which budget requests start from scratch regardless of previous appropriations.

Scheduling - A listing of necessary activities, their order of accomplishment, who is to do each, and time needed to complete them.

Gantt Chart - A bar graph with time on the horizontal axis and the activities to be scheduled on the vertical axis. The bars show output, both planned and actual, over a period of time.

Load chart - A modified Gantt chart that schedules capacity by workstations.

Program Evaluation and Review Technique (PERT) - A technique for scheduling complicated projects comprising many activities, some of which are interdependent.

> **PERT network** - A flowchartlike diagram showing the sequence of activities needed to complete a project and the time or cost associated with each.

> **Events** - End points that represent the completion of major activities in a PERT network.

> **Activities** - The time or resources needed to progress from one event to another in a PERT network.

> **Critical Path** - The longest sequence of activities in a PERT network.

Breakeven analysis - A technique for identifying the point at which total revenue is just sufficient to cover total costs.

Linear programming - A mathematical technique that solves resource allocation problems.

Queuing theory - A technique that balances the cost of having a waiting line against the cost of service to maintain that line.

Probability theory - The use of statistics to analyze past predictable patterns and to reduce risk in future plans.

Marginal analysis - A planning technique that assesses the incremental costs or revenues in a decision.

Simulation - A model of a real-world phenomenon that contains one or more variables that can be manipulated in order to assess their impact.

Time management - A personal form of scheduling time effectively.

> **Response time** - Uncontrollable time spent responding to requests, demands, and problems initiated by others.

> **Discretionary time** - The part of a manager's time that is controllable.

MULTIPLE CHOICE QUESTIONS

1. The basis for revenue forecasts is

    a. changes in the environment.
    b. historical revenue amounts.
    c. trends for revenue figures.
    d. all of the above.

2. Which of the following is an example of a qualitative forecasting technique?

    a. regression model
    b. substitution effect
    c. customer evaluation
    d. time series analysis

3. A forecasting method that applies a set of math rules to past data to predict future outcomes is

    a. sales-force competition.
    b. quantitative forecast.
    c. jury of opinion.
    d. qualitative forecast.

4. Budgets can be set for which of the following?

    a. improving time and space
    b. revenue and expenses and capital expenditures
    c. the use of material resources
    d. all of the above

5. The _____ would help reveal potential shortages or surpluses of cash.

    a. expense budget
    b. cash budget
    c. profit budget
    d. revenue budget

6. The _____ is essentially a planning device for marketing and sales activities.

    a. expense budget
    b. cash budget
    c. profit budget
    d. revenue budget

7. The _____ lists the primary activities undertaken by a division to achieve its goal and allocates a dollar amount needed for each division to operate.

    a. expense budget
    b. cash budget
    c. profit budget
    d. revenue budget

8. The _____ allows managers to forecast future needs for property, buildings, and major equipment.

   a. capital expenditure budget
   b. fixed budget
   c. variable budget
   d. cash budget

9. The _____ helps managers to better plan costs by specifying cost schedules for varying levels of income.

   a. capital expenditure budget
   b. fixed budget
   c. variable budget
   d. cash budget

10. _____ is a method that allows managers to improve quality by analyzing and then copying the methods of major competitors.

    a. Environmental scanning
    b. Forecast
    c. Benchmarking
    d. Budget

11. The _____ shifts the burden of proof to the manager to justify why her/his actions should get any budget at all.

    a. incremental budget
    b. zero-base budget
    c. revenue budget
    d. none of the above

12. This scheduling technique uses a bar graph to illustrate planned activities and their completion over a period of time:

    a. load chart
    b. Gantt chart
    c. PERT
    d. Critical Path

13. The longest time through the network for a PERT project:

    a. activity
    b. critical path
    c. event
    d. PERT network

14. A flowchart diagram that illustrates the flow of activities from start to finish:

    a. activity
    b. critical path
    c. event
    d. PERT network

15. In constructing an office building, pouring concrete for the foundation in two weeks is an example of a(n)

    a. activity
    b. critical path
    c. event
    d. PERT network

16. This linear programming formula is used to set up one of two possible desired outcomes, ie. maximize profit or minimize cost:

    a. constraints
    b. feasibility region
    c. objective function
    d. none of the above

17. A candy company produces two kinds of candy using the same ingredients and has the following available this week: 500 pounds of chocolate, 300 pounds of sugar, and 100 pounds of nuts. Managers must know these values to write the _____ for the linear programming problem.

    a. constraints
    b. feasibility region
    c. objective function
    d. none of the above

18. Using this technique, a dry cleaner who wonders whether she should take on a new customer would not consider total revenue and total costs, but rather additional revenue and costs generated by this particular order.

    a. probability theory
    b. marginal analysis
    c. simulation
    d. queuing theory

19. _____ is a model of some real world situation that is manipulated to assess the impact on a company if the situation really occurs.

    a. probability theory
    b. marginal analysis
    c. simulation
    d. queuing theory

20. Which of the following is not a step to better time management?

    a. List activities necessary to achieve objectives.
    b. Try to schedule work in the mornings.
    c. Schedule your activities according to priorities you set.
    d. Make a list of objectives and rank them according to their importance.

TRUE/FALSE QUESTIONS

1. T F Environmental scanning refers to screening large amounts of information to detect emerging trends and create a set of scenarios.

2. T F Managers in both small and large organizations are increasingly turning to environmental scanning to anticipate and interpret changes in their environment.

3. T F Environmental scanning makes forecasting unnecessary.

4. T F The basis for revenue forecasts is historical revenue figures, revenue trends, and changes in the environment.

5. T F Quantitative forecasting uses judgement and opinions of knowledgeable individuals to predict future outcomes.

6. T F In time of severe competition or recession, managers typically look first at the revenue budget to achieve economic efficiency.

7. T F The most popular approach to budgeting is the zero-base budget.

8. T F An incremental budget allocates funds to activities that are need to achieve a specific objective.

9. T F In a zero-base budget system, budget requests start from scratch, regardless of previous appropriations.

10. T F A modified Gantt Chart that schedules capacity by work stations is called PERT.

11. T F PERT allows managers to monitor a project's resources as necessary to keep the project on schedule.

12. T F Break-even analysis is a technique for identifying the point at which total revenue is just sufficient to cover fixed costs.

13. T F   Selecting transportation routes that minimize shipping costs and allocating a limited advertising budget among various product brands are two uses for linear programming technology.

14. T F   Marginal analysis is a planning technique that balances the cost of having to wait in line against the cost of service to maintain that line.

15. T F   The part of a manager's time that she can control is called response time.

MATCH TERMS WITH DEFINITIONS

a. Environmental scanning
b. Competitor intelligence
c. Scenario
d. Forecasts
e. Quantitative forecasting
f. Qualitative forecasting
g. Benchmarking
h. Simulation
i. Marginal analysis
j. Queuing theory
k. Program Evaluation and Review Technique (PERT)
l. Load chart
m. Scheduling
n. Zero-base budgeting (ZBB)
o. Budget

___ 1. A planning technique that assesses the incremental costs or revenues in a decision.

___ 2. A technique for scheduling complicated projects comprising many activities, some of which are interdependent.

___ 3. A model of a real-world phenomenon that contains one or more variables that can be manipulated in order to assess their impact.

___ 4. A system in which budget requests start from scratch regardless of previous appropriations.

___ 5. A consistent view of what the future is likely to be.

___ 6. Applies a set of mathematical rules to a series of past data to predict future outcomes.

___ 7. The search for the best practices among competitors or noncompetitors that lead to their superior performance.

___ 8. Environmental scanning activity that seeks to identify who competitors are, what they're doing, and how their actions will affect the focus organization.

___ 9. A listing of necessary activities, their order of accomplishment, who is to do each, and time needed to complete them.

___ 10. The screening of large amounts of information to detect emerging trends and create scenarios.

___ 11. Uses the judgment and opinions of knowledgeable individuals to predict future outcomes.

___ 12. A modified Gantt chart that schedules capacity by workstations.

___ 13. A numerical plan for allocating resources to specific activities.

___ 14. Predictions of future outcomes.

___ 15. A technique that balances the cost of having a waiting line against the cost of service to maintain that line.

CHAPTER 10

ORGANIZATION STRUCTURE AND DESIGN

Chapter Objectives

1. Define organization structure and organization design.

2. Explain why structure and design are important to an organization.

3. Describe the vertical dimensions of organizations, including unity of command, span of control, authority-responsibility, and centralization-decentralization.

4. Explain the horizontal dimensions of organizations, including division of labor and types of departmentalization.

5. Compare and contrast the various types of departmentalization, including functional, product customer, geographic, and process.

6. Describe cross-functional teams and matrix organizations.

7. Identify the various contingency factors that influence organization design.

8. Describe current organizational designs.

9. Explain why organizations are using team-based structures.

10. Describe the boundaryless organization and the factors that have contributed to its development.

Chapter Outline

I. Defining Organization Structure and Design

II. Building the Vertical Dimension of Organizations

    A. Unity of Command

        1. The Classical View

        2. The Contemporary View

B. Authority and Responsibility

   1. The Classical View

   2. The Contemporary View

C. Span of Control

   1. The Classical View

   2. The Contemporary View

D. Centralization and Decentralization

   1. The Classical View

   2. The Contemporary View

III. Building the Horizontal Dimension of Organizations

A. Division of Labor

   1. The Classical View

   2. The Contemporary View

B. Departmentalization

   1. The Classical View

   2. The Contemporary View

IV. The Contingency Approach to Organization Design

A. Mechanistic and Organic Organizations

B. Strategy and Structure

C. Size and Structure

D. Technology and Structure

   1. Joan Woodward

   2. Charles Perrow

   3. What's our conclusion?

E. Environment and Structure

V. Applications of Organization Design

    A. Simple Structure

    B. Bureaucracy

    C. Team-Base Structures

    D. The Boundaryless Organization

Key Terms

Organizing - The process of creating an organization's structure.

Organization structure - An organization's framework as expressed by its degree of complexity, formalization, and centralization.

    Complexity - The amount of differentiation in an organization.

    Formalization - The degree to which an organization relies on rules and procedures to direct the behavior of employees.

    Centralization - The concentration of decision-making authority to lower levels in an organization.

Organization design - The development or changing of an organization's structure.

Unity of command - The principle that a subordinate should have one and only one superior to whom he or she is directly responsible.

Authority - The rights inherent in a managerial position to give orders and expect them to be obeyed.

Responsibility - An obligation to perform assigned activities.

Line authority - The authority that entitles a manager to direct the work of a subordinate.

Chain of command - The flow of authority from the top to the bottom of an organization.

Staff authority - Authority given to individuals who support, assist, and advise others who have line authority.

Acceptance theory of authority - The theory that authority comes from the willingness of subordinates to accept.

Power - The capacity to influence decisions.

Span of control - The number of subordinates a manager can supervise efficiently and effectively.

Empowerment - A managerial approach in which employees are given substantial authority and say to make decisions on their own.

Departmentalization - The process of grouping individuals into separate units or departments to accomplish organizational goals.

>**Functional departmentalization** - Grouping activities by functions performed.
>
>**Product departmentalization** - Grouping activities by product line.
>
>**Customer departmentalization** - Grouping activities on the basis of common customers.
>
>**Geographic departmentalization** - Grouping activities on the basis of territory or geographic area.
>
>**Process departmentalization** - Grouping activities on the basis of product or customer flow.

Cross-functional team - An organizational arrangement in which a hybrid grouping of individuals who are experts in various specialties (or functions) work together.

Matrix organization - An organizing approach that assigns specialists from different functional departments to work on one or more projects that are led by a project manager.

Mechanistic organization (bureaucracy) - A structure that is high in complexity, formalization, and centralization.

Organic organization (adhocracy) - A structure that is low in complexity, formalization, and centralization.

Unit production - The production of items in units or small batches.

Mass production - Large-batch manufacturing.

Process production - Continuous-process production.

Task variability - The number of exceptions people encounter in their work.

Problem analyzability - The type of search procedures employees follow in responding to exceptions.

Simple structure - An organizational design that is low in complexity and formalization high in centralization.

Functional structure - An organizational design that groups similar or related occupational specialties together.

Divisional structure - An organization structure made up of autonomous self-contained units.

Team-based structure - An organization structure made up of work groups or teams that perform that organization's work.

Boundaryless organization - An organization whose design is not defined by, or limited to, the boundaries imposed by a predefined structure.

MULTIPLE CHOICE QUESTIONS

1. The formalization of organization structure

    a. considers where the decision-making authority lies.
    b. is the degree to which an organization relies on rules and procedures to direct the behavior of employees.
    c. considers how much differentiation there is in an organization.
    d. all of the above.

2. The complexity of organization structure

    a. considers where the decision-making authority lies.
    b. is the degree to which an organization relies on rules and procedures to direct the behavior of employees.
    c. considers how much differentiation there is in an organization.
    d. all of the above.

3. A manager decides that she/he can manage more people and creates several new departments in her/his chain of command, she/he is utilizing the organizational principle of

    a. unity of command.
    b. division of labor.
    c. span of control.
    d. centralization.

4. The organizational principle of _____ is being illustrated when an employee answers to one boss who gives him orders related to his job.

    a. unity of command.
    b. division of labor.
    c. span of control.
    d. centralization.

5. Which is not true for the classical view of authority?

   a. Managers are not the only people in organizations with power.
   b. Responsibility cannot be delegated.
   c. Managers should delegate downward to subordinates, giving them prescribed limits within which they must operate.
   d. Authority and responsibility are related.

6. An auto manufacturer that divides the company into departments according to different models of automobiles uses _____ departmentalization.

   a. product
   b. customer
   c. function
   d. process

7. A book publishing company that has several divisions such as children's books, adult novels, and college textbooks uses _____ departmentalization.

   a. product
   b. customer
   c. function
   d. process

8. A bookcase manufacturer that has several departments such as wood cutting, staining, and assembly uses _____ departmentalization.

   a. product
   b. customer
   c. function
   d. process

9. A fast food organization that maintains a central office for marketing, accounting, and personnel uses _____ departmentalization.

   a. product
   b. customer
   c. function
   d. process

10. Classic theorists advocated that organization structures for all organizations should have

    a. low complexity, high formalization, high centralization.
    b. high complexity, low formalization, high centralization.
    c. high complexity, high formalization, high centralization.
    d. high complexity, high formalization, low centralization.

11. The mechanistic organization is also referred to as a(n)

    a. adhocracy.
    b. bureaucracy.
    c. organic structure.
    d. decentralized structure.

12. The mass-production technology category in Joan Woodward's research is defined as

    a. continuous process production.
    b. large-batch manufacturing.
    c. tailor made products.
    d. production of items in units or small batches.

13. According to Joan Woodward, the most effective structure for unit and process production is

    a. bureaucracy.
    b. mechanistic.
    c. organic.
    d. There is no one "best" structure choice for these technologies.

14. A type of technology in Charles Perrow's study that has a large number of exception, but the exceptions can be handled in a rational and systematic manner is

    a. routine.
    b. engineering.
    c. craft.
    d. nonroutine.

15. A type of technology in Charles Perrow's study that has many exception and it is difficult to analyze problems is

    a. routine.
    b. engineering.
    c. craft.
    d. nonroutine.

16. Which is not true for functional structures?

    a. A strength is the advantage that occurs from specialization.
    b. A weakness is that the organization frequently loses sight of its best interests in the pursuit of functional goals.
    c. It provides good training for future chief executives.
    d. It is a mechanistic approach to structure.

17. A disadvantage of divisional structures is

    a. There is a focus on results.
    b. Activities and resources are duplicated.
    c. Divisional structures require much involvement by top managers.
    d. It is difficult to develop senior level managers in divisional structures.

18. An example of this structure is when Kellogg's company temporarily brings together people who have expertise in product design, food research, marketing, finance, and manufacturing to plan and design new cereals.

    a. matrix.
    b. network.
    c. task force.
    d. committee.

19. The Massachusetts office of Canadian Company, Sun Life Assurance have organized their customer representatives into groups of eight who are trained to handle all customers' requests. The company is using a _____ structure.

    a. divisional
    b. team-based structure
    c. boundaryless organizational
    d. simple

20. Which is not a disadvantage of a matrix structure?

    a. A matrix structure often creates confusion.
    b. There is a tendency for power struggles in the organization.
    c. Coordination is difficult.
    d. There is less duplication of specialized resources than in product departmentalization.

TRUE/FALSE QUESTIONS

1. T F   The degree to which an organization relies on rules and procedures to direct the behavior of employees is called complexity.

2. T F   When managers construct or change an organization structure, they are involved in organization design.

3. T F   Assembly line production is an example of division of labor.

4. T F   When managers delegate authority, they must also allocate responsibility.

5. T F   Line authority is the authority that supports, assists, and advises holders of staff authority.

6. T F   Setting up departments by separating engineering, accounting, manufacturing, personnel, and marketing departments is functional departmentalization.

7. T F   Organizations that must change rapidly in response to environmental change, need mechanistic structures.

8. T F   In the real world, there are few purely mechanistic or purely organic organizations.

9. T F   Making organization design decisions is a universal activity for all managers.

10. T F   Mechanistic design options include simple, matrix, network, task force, and committee structures.

11. T F   An obvious weakness of a functional structure is that the organization frequently loses sight of its best interests in the pursuit of functional goals.

12. T F   The divisional framework crates a set of autonomous "little companies".

13. T F   An advantage of divisional structure is that activities and resources are not duplicated.

14. T F   The simple structure is the most widely practiced in small businesses in which the manager and the owner are one and the same.

15. T F   The matrix structure breaks the unity of command principle.

MATCH TERMS WITH DEFINITIONS

a. Organic Organization (adhocracy)
b. Organization structure
c. Complexity
d. Formalization
e. Centralization
f. Organization design
g. Unity of command
h. Authority
i. Chain of command
j. Span of control
k. Empowerment
l. Departmentalization
m. Cross-functional team

n. Matrix organization
o. Mechanistic organization (bureaucracy)

___ 1. The amount of differentiation in an organization.

___ 2. The number of subordinates a manager can supervise efficiently and effectively.

___ 3. The development or changing of an organization's structure.

___ 4. The degree to which an organization relies on rules and procedures to direct the behavior of employees.

___ 5. The rights inherent in a managerial position to give orders and expect them to be obeyed.

___ 6. The concentration of decision-making authority to lower levels in an organization.

___ 7. The flow of authority from the top to the bottom of an organization.

___ 8. A structure that is low in complexity, formalization, and centralization.

___ 9. A managerial approach in which employees are given substantial authority and say to make decisions on their own.

___ 10. An organization's framework as expressed by its degree of complexity, formalization, and centralization.

___ 11. An organizational arrangement in which a hybrid grouping of individuals who are experts in various specialties (or functions) work together.

___ 12. The principle that a subordinate should have one and only one superior to whom he or she is directly responsible.

___ 13. An organizing approach that assigns specialists from different functional departments to work on one or more projects that are led by a project manager.

___ 14. A structure that is high in complexity, formalization, and centralization.

___ 15. The process of grouping individuals into separate units or departments to accomplish organizational goals.

CHAPTER 11

HUMAN RESOURCE MANAGEMENT

Chapter Objectives

1. Describe the human resource management process.

2. Discuss the influence of government regulations on human resource decisions.

3. Differentiate between job descriptions and job specifications.

4. Contrast recruitment and decruitment options.

5. Explain the importance of validity and reliability in selection.

6. Describe the selection devices that work best with various kinds of jobs.

7. Identify the various training methods.

8. Outline the five stages in a career.

9. Describe the various types of compensation and how compensation decisions are made.

10. Describe how HRM practices can facilitate workforce diversity.

11. Explain why sexual harassment is a growing concern of management.

12. Discuss how organizations are meeting the challenges of employee family concerns, SIDA in the workplace, and maintaining morale after downsizing.

Chapter Outline

I. Managers and Human Resources Departments

II. The Human Resource Management Process

III. Important Environmental Considerations

    A. Major U.S. Federal Laws and Regulations

IV. Human Resource Planning

    A. Current Assessment

    B. Future Assessment

    C. Developing a Future Program

V. Recruitment and Decruitment

    A. Major Sources of Potential Job Candidates

VI. Selection

    A. What is Selection?

        1. Prediction

        2. Validity

        3. Reliability

    B. Selection Devices

        1. The Application form

        2. Written tests

        3. Performance simulation tests

        4. Interviews

            a. Suggestions for interviewing

        5. Background Investigation

        6. Physical Examination

    C. What Works Best and When?

VII. Orientation

VIII. Employee Training

    A. Skill Categories

        1. Technical

        2. Interpersonal

3. Problem Solving

B. Training Methods

1. On-the-Job Training

2. Off-the-Job Training

IX. Career Development

A. Career Stages

1. Exploration

2. Establishment

3. Midcareer

4. Late career

5. Decline

6. Applying the Career Stage Model

X. Keys to a Successful Management Career

A. Select Your First Job Judiciously

B. Do Good Work

C. Present the Right Image

D. Learn the Power Structure

E. Gain Control of Organizational Resources

F. Stay Visible

G. Don't Stay Too Long in Your First Job

H. Support Your Boss

I. Stay Mobile

J. Think Laterally

K. Think of Your Career in Terms of Skills You're Acquiring and Continue Upgrading Those Skill.

       L. Work Harder Than Ever at Developing a Network

XI. Compensation and Benefits

XII. Current Issues in Human Resource Management

       A. Managing Workforce Diversity

           1. Recruitment

           2. Selection

           3. Orientation and Training

       B. Sexual Harassment

       C. Family Concerns

       D. AIDS in the Workplace

       E. Downsizing

Key Terms

Human resource process - Activities necessary for staffing the organization and sustaining high employee performance.

Labor union - An organization that represents workers and seeks to protect their interests through collective bargaining.

Labor-management relations - The formal interactions between unions and an organization's management.

Bona fide occupational qualifications (BFOQ) - A criterion such as sex, age, or national origin may be used as a basis for hiring if it can be clearly demonstrated to be job related.

Affirmative action programs - Programs that enhance the organizational status of members of protected groups.

Human resource planning - The process by which management ensures that it has the right personnel, who are capable of completing those tasks that help the organization reach its objectives.

Job analysis - An assessment that defines jobs and the behaviors necessary to perform them.

Job description - A written statement of what a jobholder does, how it is done, and why it is done.

Job specification - A statement of the minimum acceptable qualifications that an incumbent must possess to perform a given job successfully.

Recruitment - The process of locating, identifying, and attracting capable applicants.

Decruitment - Techniques for reducing the labor supply within an organization.

Selection process - The process of screening job applicants to ensure that the most appropriate candidates are hired.

> **Validity** - The proven relationship that exists between a selection device and some relevant criterion.
>
> **Reliability** - The ability of a selection device to measure the same thing consistently.
>
> **Work sampling** - A personnel selection device in which job applicants are presented with a miniature replica of a job and are asked to perform tasks central to that job.
>
> **Assessment centers** - Places in which job candidates undergo performance simulation tests that evaluate managerial potential.

Orientation - The introduction of a new employee into his or her job and the organization.

Job rotation - On-the-job training that involves lateral transfers in which employees get to work at different jobs.

Mentor - A person who sponsors or supports another employee who is lower in the organization.

Vestibule training - Training in which employees learn on the same equipment they will be using but in a simulated work environment.

Career - The sequence of positions occupied by a person during the course of a lifetime.

Realistic job preview - Exposing job candidates to both negative and positive information about a job and an organization.

Sexual harassment - Behavior marked by sexually aggressive remarks, unwanted touching and sexual advances, requests for sexual favors, or other verbal or physical conduct of a sexual nature.

MULTIPLE CHOICE QUESTIONS

1. The activities in human resource planning include

    a. orientation and training.
    b. human resource planning.
    c. identifying and correcting performance problems and helping employees sustain a high level of performance.
    d. all of the above.

2. Programs that enhance the organizational status of members of protected groups are

    a. affirmative action programs.
    b. bonafide occupational qualifications.
    c. collective bargaining agreements.
    d. all of the above.

3. Agreements that usually define such things as recruitment sources, criteria for hiring, and disciplinary practices are

    a. affirmative action programs.
    b. bonafide occupational qualifications.
    c. collective bargaining agreements.
    d. all of the above.

4. Criterion such as sex, age, or national origin that may be used as a basis for hiring if it can be clearly demonstrated to be job related are

    a. affirmative action programs.
    b. bonafide occupational qualifications.
    c. collective bargaining agreements.
    d. all of the above.

5. During the 1960s and 1970s, the number of federal laws related to human resource management

    a. decreased.
    b. increased slightly.
    c. increased dramatically.
    d. remained about the same.

6. Human resource planning includes

    a. assessing future human needs.
    b. assessing current human resources.
    c. developing a program to meet future human resource needs.
    d. all of the above.

7. A human resource inventory is

   a. employee education, training, prior employment, languages spoken, capabilities, and specialized skills of employees.
   b. a statement of what a jobholder does and how it is done.
   c. an assessment that defines jobs and the behaviors necessary to perform them.
   d. a statement of minimum acceptable qualifications for job candidates.

8. The _____ for a janitor includes: Job Class 4 and the duties are to clean the offices and hallways of the building by vacuuming, dusting, and mopping once each week.

   a. job analysis
   b. job specification
   c. human resource inventory
   d. job description

9. In setting up operations for a new production company, the personnel manager and area managers have developed a list of jobs needed and numbers of people needed for each job. This is a

   a. job analysis
   b. job specification
   c. human resource inventory
   d. job description

10. A study in the company revealed that 40% of workers have college degrees, 20% have worked at the company for five years or more, and 25% have been trained in the use of computers.

    a. job analysis
    b. job specification
    c. human resource inventory
    d. job description

11. The advertised skills needed for a computer programmer include: college degree, two years experience using an IBM main frame computer, and training on CAD computer software. this describes a

    a. job analysis
    b. job specification
    c. human resource inventory
    d. job description

12. The process of locating, identifying, and attracting capable applicants is called

    a. decruitment.
    b. orientation.
    c. recruitment.
    d. selection.

13. Layoffs and reduced workweeks are examples of

    a. decruitment.
    b. orientation.
    c. recruitment.
    d. selection.

14. Screening job applicants to ensure that the most appropriate candidates are hired is called

    a. decruitment.
    b. orientation.
    c. recruitment.
    d. selection.

15. A source of potential job candidates that is low in cost and helps build employee morale is

    a. employee referrals.
    b. internal search.
    c. public employment agencies.
    d. private employment agencies.

16. If this source of potential job candidates is used, the available candidates tend to be unskilled or minimally skilled.

    a. employee referrals.
    b. internal search.
    c. public employment agencies.
    d. private employment agencies.

17. In selection, when a job candidate is selected, but performs poorly there is

    a. validity.
    b. accept error.
    c. reliability.
    d. reject error.

18. The proven relationship that exists between a selection device and some relevant criterion is

   a. validity.
   b. accept error.
   c. reliability.
   d. reject error.

19. An employee has taken a job skills test three times and scored very differently each time. This suggests that there is a problem with

   a. validity.
   b. accept error.
   c. reliability.
   d. reject error.

20. An assessment center is one method often used for this selection device:

   a. application form.
   b. interview.
   c. background investigation.
   d. performance simulation test.

TRUE/FALSE QUESTIONS

1. T F Whether or not an organization has a personnel department, every manager is involved with human resource decisions in her/his unit.

2. T F A bona fide occupational qualification allows managers to use criteria such as sex, age, or national origin as a basis for hiring, without proving a need for selection based on this criteria.

3. T F Human resource planning can be expressed in two parts: assessing current human resources and assessing future human resource needs.

4. T F A job specification is a written statement of what a jobholder does, how it is done, and why it is done.

5. T F The greater the skill required or the higher the position in the organization hierarchy, the more the recruitment process will expand to become a regional or national search.

6. T F Some options for decruitment include firing, layoffs, and attrition.

7. T F   Obvious costs to the organization for "accept" errors include increased selection costs and discrimination charges.

8. T F   Organizations have been using tests more frequently as a selection device since the 1960's.

9. T F   Work sampling is a personnel selection device in which job applicants are presented with a miniature replica of a job and are allowed to perform tasks central to that job.

10. T F   The major objective of orientation is to begin job training.

11. T F   Most training is directed at upgrading and improving an employee's technical skills.

12. T F   Classroom lectures, films and simulation exercises are various kinds of on-the-job training.

13. T F   Evidence indicates that acquiring a mentor who is part of the organization power core is essential for managers who aspire to make it to the top.

14. T F   A worker's compensation can be influenced on the level of labor or capital intensity the organization experiences.

15. T F   The courts have ruled that if an employee who is guilty of sexual harassment is a superior or agent for an organization, then the organization is liable for sexual harassment, regardless of whether the act was authorized or forbidden by the organization or whether the organization knew of the act.

MATCH TERMS WITH DEFINITIONS

a. Job rotation
b. Vestibule training
c. Sexual harassment
d. Bona fide occupational qualifications (BFOQ)
e. Affirmative action programs
f. Job analysis
g. Job description
h. Job specification
i. Recruitment
j. Decruitment
k. Selection process
l. Validity
m. Reliability
n. Work sampling
o. Assessment centers

106

___ 1. A written statement of what a jobholder does, how it is done, and why it is done.

___ 2. The ability of a selection device to measure the same thing consistently.

___ 3. A statement of the minimum acceptable qualifications that an incumbent must possess to perform a given job successfully.

___ 4. The process of locating, identifying, and attracting capable applicants.

___ 5. Programs that enhance the organizational status of members of protected groups.

___ 6. Places in which job candidates undergo performance simulation tests that evaluate managerial potential.

___ 7. A criterion such as sex, age, or national origin may be used as a basis for hiring if it can be clearly demonstrated to be job related.

___ 8. Training in which employees learn on the same equipment they will be using but in a simulated work environment.

___ 9. Techniques for reducing the labor supply within an organization.

___ 10. The process of screening job applicants to ensure that the most appropriate candidates are hired.

___ 11. Behavior marked by sexually aggressive remarks, unwanted touching and sexual advances, requests for sexual favors, or other verbal or physical conduct of a sexual nature.

___ 12. An assessment that defines jobs and the behaviors necessary to perform them.

___ 13. The proven relationship that exists between a selection device and some relevant criterion.

___ 14. On-the-job training that involves lateral transfers in which employees get to work at different jobs.

___ 15. A personnel selection device in which job applicants are presented with a miniature replica of a job and are asked to perform tasks central to that job.

CHAPTER 12

MANAGING CHANGE AND INNOVATION

Chapter Objectives

1. Contrast the "calm waters" and "white-water rapids" metaphors of change.

2. Explain why people are likely to resist change.

3. List techniques for reducing resistance to change.

4. Describe what managers can change in organizations.

5. Describe the situational factors that facilitate cultural change.

6. Explain how management should go about enacting cultural change.

7. Describe how managers can implement TQM.

8. Explain how re-engineering relates to change.

9. Describe techniques for reducing employee stress.

10. Explain how organizations can stimulate innovation.

Chapter Outline

I. What is Change:

II. Forces for Change

    A. External Forces

    B. Internal Forces

    C. The Manager as Change Agent

III. Two Different Views on the Change Process

    A. The "Calm Waters" Metaphor

        1. Kurtewin - Unfreezing, changing, refreezing

        1. Kurt Lewin - Unfreezing, changing, refreezing

   B. The "White-Water Rapids" Metaphor

   C. Putting the Two Views in Perspective

IV. Organizational Inertia and Resistance to Change

   A. Resistance to Change

   B. Techniques for Reducing Resistance

        1. Education and Communication

        2. Participation

        3. Facilitation and Support

        4. Negotiation

        5. Manipulation and Cooptation

        6. Coercion

   C. Techniques for Managing Change

        1. Changing Structure

        2. Changing Technology

        3. Changing People

            a. Sensitivity training

            b. Survey feedback

            c. Process consultation

            d. Team building

V. Contemporary Issues in Managing Change

   A. Changing Organizational Cultures

        1. Understanding the Situational Factors

        2. How can Cultural Change be Accomplished?

    B. Implementing TQM

        1. Focusing the Change Effort

        2. Role of the Change Agent

    C. Re-engineering

    D. Handling Employee Stress

        1. What is Stress?

        2. Causes of Stress

        3. Symptoms of Stress

        4. Reducing Stress

VI. Stimulating Innovation

    A. Innovation Versus Creativity

    B. Fostering Innovation

        1. Structural Variables

        2. Cultural Variables

        3. Human Resource Variables

Key Terms

Change - An alteration in people, structure, or technology.

Change agents - People who act as catalysts and manage the change process.

Organization development (OD) - Techniques to change people and the quality of interpersonal work relationships.

    Sensitivity training - A method of changing behavior through unstructured group interaction.

    Survey feedback - A technique for assessing attitudes, identifying discrepancies between these attitudes and perceptions, and resolving the differences by using survey information feedback groups.

Process consultation - Help given by an outside consultant to a manager in perceiving, understanding, and acting on process events.

Team building - Interaction among members of work teams to learn how each member thinks and works.

Intergroup development - Changing the attitudes, stereotypes, and perceptions that work groups have of each other.

Stress - A dynamic condition in which an individual is confronted with an opportunity, constraint, or demand related to what he or she desires and for which the outcome is perceived to be both uncertain and important.

Type A behavior - Behavior marked by a chronic sense of time urgency and an excessive competitive drive.

Type B behavior - Behavior that is relaxed, easygoing, and noncompetitive.

Creativity - The ability to combine ideas in a unique way or to make unusual associations between ideas.

Innovation - The process of taking a creative idea and turning it into a useful product, service, or method of operation.

MULTIPLE CHOICE QUESTIONS

1. Which is not an external force for change?

    a. employee attitudes
    b. laws and regulations
    c. technology
    d. economic changes

2. Which is not an internal force for change?

    a. work force changes
    b. employee attitudes
    c. strategy changes
    d. economic changes

3. Outside consultants are sometimes hired as a change agent because

   a. they do not understand the organization history.
   b. they offer an objective perspective.
   c. they do not have to live with the repercussions after change is implemented.
   d. they do not understand organization culture and operating procedures.

4. An example of the _____ part of Lewin's model of change is a worker who accepts the new equipment he uses as the best approach to his job.

   a. change
   b. refreeze
   c. driving force
   d. unfreeze

5. A worker attends a seminar related to the use of computer technology in production. This seminar causes the worker to investigate how the technology could be used in his company. The part of Lewin's model that includes this action is

   a. change.
   b. refreeze.
   c. driving force.
   d. unfreeze.

6. An example of the _____ part of Lewin's model of change is a worker who begins to question the use of traditional methods for production that the company has used for thirty years.

   a. change
   b. refreeze
   c. driving force
   d. unfreeze

7. Why do people resist change?

   a. concern over personal loss
   b. uncertainty
   c. belief that the change is not in the organization's best interest.
   d. all of the above.

8. The most important method for reducing resistance to change when there is much fear and anxiety about the change is

   a. education and communication.
   b. participation.
   c. support.
   d. negotiation.

9. A technique for assessing attitudes, identifying discrepancies in them, and resolving the differences by using information collected through questionnaires in discussions with groups is called

    a. sensitivity training.
    b. team building.
    c. survey feedback.
    d. process consultation

10. Which of the following should stimulate creativity in an organization?

    a. acceptance of ambiguity
    b. focus on ends rather than means
    c. tolerance of risk
    d. all of the above

11. A process of taking an idea and turning it into a useful product, service, or method or operation is

    a. change
    b. creativity
    c. innovation
    d. intergroup development

12. Changing the attitudes, stereotypes, and perceptions that work groups have of each other is

    a. change
    b. creativity
    c. innovation
    d. intergroup development

13. The ability to combine ideas in a unique way or make unusual associations between ideas is

    a. change
    b. creativity
    c. innovation
    d. intergroup development

14. Which is not a characteristic of the structure of an organization that expects to implement TQM?

    a. wider span of control
    b. decentralized decision making
    c. increased division of labor
    d. reduced vertical differentiation

15. Which is not a characteristic of the work force that is committed to TQM?

    a. skilled in problem-solving techniques
    b. individual problem-solving
    c. team work
    d. commitment to quality and continual improvement

16. A person who is relaxed and noncompetitive:

    a. Type A behavior
    b. Type B behavior
    c. stress
    d. stressor

17. Examples of _____ are job dissatisfaction and personal problems.

    a. Type A behavior
    b. Type B behavior
    c. stress
    d. stressor

18. A person who is competitive and impatient:

    a. Type A behavior
    b. Type B behavior
    c. stress
    d. stressor

19. Reengineering can be characterized as a

    a. "calm waters" change.
    b. "a white-water rapids" change.
    c. second step in a change process.
    d. type of TQM.

20. Which is not a favorable condition that might facilitate cultural change in an organization?

    a. new leadership
    b. small and young organization
    c. consistent operations over time
    d. weak culture

TRUE/FALSE QUESTIONS

1. T F   Handling change is an integral part of every manager's job.

2. T F   Both external and internal factors create a need for change in organizations.

3. T F   The change agent in the organization should be the manager of the company.

4. T F   According to Kurt Lewin, successful change involves unfreezing the old behavior and attempting a new behavior.

5. T F   Computer software manufacturers can safely use the "calm waters" metaphor with regard to change.

6. T F   People resist change because of uncertainty, concern over personal loss, and the belief that the change is not in the organization's best interest.

7. T F   Negotiation is necessary to reduce resistance to change when there is misinformation.

8. T F   Facilitation and support are necessary to reduce resistance to change when there is much anxiety about the change.

9. T F   OD is a method of changing behavior through unstructured group interaction.

10. T F   Research evidence indicates that sensitivity training has very few disadvantages and is almost always successful

11. T F   The fact that an organization culture is made of relatively stable and permanent characteristics tends to make the culture very resistant to change.

12. T F   When managers talk about changing an organization to make it more creative, they usually mean that they want to stimulate innovation.

13. T F   Organizations that foster innovation are intolerant of employee risk taking.

14. T F   Organizations that need to make dramatic, radical changes in operations may need to use TQM as the second phase in a two-phase change process, rather than the first phase.

15. T F   Stress in itself is undesirable.

MATCH TERMS WITH DEFINITIONS

a. Type B behavior
b. Type A behavior
c. Organization development (OD)
d. Creativity
e. Innovation
f. Intergroup development
g. Sensitivity training
h. Stress
i. Change agents
j. Change
k. Survey feedback
l. Team building
m. Process consultation

___ 1. Techniques to change people and the quality of interpersonal work relationships.

___ 2. The process of taking a creative idea and turning it into a useful product, service, or method of operation.

___ 3. Changing the attitudes, stereotypes, and perceptions that work groups have of each other.

___ 4. A technique for assessing attitudes, identifying discrepancies between these attitudes and perceptions, and resolving the differences by using survey information feedback groups.

___ 5. Interaction among members of work teams to learn how each member thinks and works.

___ 6. People who act as catalysts and manage the change process.

___ 7. A dynamic condition in which an individual is confronted with an opportunity, constraint, or demand related to what he or she desires and for which the outcome is perceived to be both uncertain and important.

___ 8. Behavior marked by a chronic sense of time urgency and an excessive competitive drive.

___ 9. An alteration in people, structure, or technology.

___ 10. Help given by an outside consultant to a manager in perceiving, understanding, and acting on process events.

___ 11. A method of changing behavior through unstructured group interaction.

___ 12. Behavior that is relaxed, easygoing, and noncompetitive.

___ 13. The ability to combine ideas in a unique way or to make unusual associations between ideas.

CHAPTER 13

FOUNDATIONS OF BEHAVIOR

Chapter Objectives

1. Define the focus and goals of organizational behavior.

2. Explain how an organization is like an iceberg.

3. Describe the three components of an attitude.

4. Identify the role that consistency plays in attitudes.

5. Explain the relationship between satisfaction and productivity.

6. Describe the Myers-Briggs personality type framework and its use in organizations.

7. Explain Holland's personality-job fit theory.

8. Describe attribution theory.

9. Identify the types of shortcuts managers use in judging others.

10. Explain how managers can shape employee behavior.

Chapter Outline

I. Toward Explaining and Predicting Behavior

    A. Focus of Organizational Behavior

    B. Goals of Organizational Behavior

II. Attitudes

    A. Attitudes and Consistency

    B. Cognitive Dissonance Theory

    C. Attitude Surveys

    D. The Satisfaction-Productivity Controversy
    E. Implications for Managers

III. Personality

    A. Predicting Behavior from Personality Traits

        1. Locus of Control

        2. Authoritarianism

        3. Machiavellianism

        4. Self-Esteem

        5. Self-Monitoring

        6. Risk-taking

    B. Personality Assessment Tests

    C. Personality Types in Different National Cultures

    D. Matching Personalities and Jobs

    E. Implications for Managers

IV. Perception

    A. Factors Influencing Perception

    B. Attribution Theory

    C. Frequently Used Shortcuts in Judging Others

    D. Implications for Managers

V. Learning

    A. Operant Conditioning

    B. Social Learning

    C. Shaping: A Managerial Tool

    D. Implications for Managers

Key Terms

Behavior - The actions of people.

Organizational behavior - The study of the actions of people at work.

Attitudes - Evaluative statements concerning objects, people, or events.

> **Cognitive component of an attitude** - The beliefs, opinions, knowledge, or information held by a person.

> **Affective component of an attitude** - the emotional or feeling segment of an attitude.

> **Behavioral component of an attitude** - An intention to behave in a certain way toward someone or something.

Job satisfaction - A person's general attitude toward his or her job.

Job involvement - The degree to which an employee identifies with his or her job, actively participates in it, and considers his or her job performance important to his or her self-worth.

Organizational commitment - An employee's orientation toward the organization in terms of his or her loyalty to, identification with, and involvement in the organization.

Cognitive dissonance - Any incompatibility between two or more attitudes or between behavior and attitudes.

Attitude surveys - Eliciting responses from employees through questionnaires about how they feel about their jobs, work groups, supervisors, and/or the organization.

Personality - A combination of psychological traits that classifies a person.

Authoritarianism - A measure of a person's belief that there should be status and power differences among people in organizations.

Machiavellianism - A measure of the degree to which people are pragmatic, maintain emotional distance, and believe that ends can justify means.

Self-esteem - An individual's degree of like or dislike for himself or herself.

Self-monitoring - a personality trait that measures an individual's ability to adjust his or her behavior to external situational factors.

Perception - The process of organizing and interpreting sensory impressions in order to give meaning to the environment.

Attribution theory - A theory used to develop explanations of how we judge people differently depending on the meaning we attribute to a given behavior.

Fundamental attribution error - The tendency to underestimate the influence of external factors and overestimate the influence of internal factors when making judgments about the behavior of others.

Self-serving bias - The tendency for individuals to attribute their own successes to internal factors while putting the blame for failures on external factors.

Selectivity - The process by which people assimilate certain bits and pieces of what they observe, depending on their interests, background, and attitudes.

Assumed similarity - The belief that others are like oneself.

Stereotyping - Judging a person on the basis of one's perception of a group to which he or she belongs.

Halo effect - A general impression of an individual based on a single characteristic.

Learning - Any relatively permanent change in behavior that occurs as a result of experience.

Operant conditioning - A type of conditioning in which desired voluntary behavior leads to a reward or prevents a punishment.

Social learning theory - People can learn through observation and direct experience.

Shaping behavior - Systematically reinforcing each successive step that moves an individual closer to the desired response.

MULTIPLE QUESTIONS

1. Organizational Behavior is

    a. a descriptive field of study with goals to explain and predict behavior.
    b. concerned with a study of the action of people at work.
    c. focuses on individual and group behavior.
    d. all of the above.

2. Evaluative statements concerning people, objects, or events are called

    a. perceptions.
    b. attitudes.
    c. personality.
    d. dissonance.

3. A process of organizing and interpreting sensory impressions in order to give meaning to the environment is called

   a. perceptions.
   b. attitudes.
   c. personality.
   d. dissonance.

4. Job satisfaction, job involvement, and organization commitment are job related examples of

   a. perceptions.
   b. attitudes.
   c. personality.
   d. dissonance.

5. Inconsistencies that cannot be avoided, but can be rationalized and justified are called

   a. perceptions.
   b. attitudes.
   c. personality.
   d. dissonance.

6. Locus of control, authoritarianism, Machiavellianism, and risk propensity are organization examples of

   a. perceptions.
   b. attitudes.
   c. personality.
   d. dissonance.

7. A worker who has an attitude that "the ends justify the means" is high in

   a. authoritarianism.
   b. risk propensity.
   c. locus of control.
   d. Machiavellianism.

8. A worker who is not willing to take chances is low in

   a. authoritarianism.
   b. risk propensity.
   c. locus of control.
   d. Machiavellianism.

9. Workers who believe that their lives are controlled by others have external

    a. authoritarianism.
    b. risk propensity.
    c. locus of control.
    d. Machiavellianism.

10. People perceive things differently because of

    a. past experiences and expectations.
    b. attitudes and motives.
    c. personality.
    d. all of the above.

11. Judging people on the basis of our perception of the group to which they belong is

    a. selectivity.
    b. stereotyping.
    c. assumed similarity.
    d. halo effect.

12. An intention to act in a certain way toward someone or something is

    a. behavioral component of an attitude.
    b. cognitive component of an attitude.
    c. affective component of an attitude.
    d. cognitive dissonance.

13. The beliefs, opinions, knowledge, or information held by a person is

    a. behavioral component of an attitude.
    b. cognitive component of an attitude.
    c. affective component of an attitude.
    d. cognitive dissonance.

14. Which is true for the satisfaction-productivity controversy?

    a. The positive relationship between satisfaction and productivity is strong.
    b. The satisfaction-productivity relationship is stronger when the employee behavior is constrained by outside forces.
    c. Satisfaction-productivity correlations are stronger for higher level employees than for lower level employees.
    d. Satisfaction leads to productivity rather than the other way around.

15. _____ is learning by direct observation and by experience.

    a. Operant conditioning
    b. Selectivity
    c. Shaping
    d. Social learning theory

16. _____ molding workers by guiding their learning in graduated steps.

    a. Operant conditioning
    b. Selectivity
    c. Shaping
    d. Social learning theory

17. Suspending an employee for two days because he is consistently late to work is an example of the following way to shape behavior.

    a. positive reinforcement
    b. extinction
    c. negative reinforcement
    d. punishment

18. Criticizing an employee in front of others for being late to work is an example of

    a. positive reinforcement
    b. extinction
    c. negative reinforcement
    d. punishment

19. The Myers-Briggs Type Indicator (MBTI) does not include which of the following as one of its four dimensions.

    a. Locus of control
    b. Preference for gathering data
    c. Style of making decisions
    d. Social interaction

20. National cultures

    a. differ in terms of degree to which people believe they can control their environment.
    b. differ in the way people respond to power and authoritarianism.
    c. differ in terms of locus of control issues.
    d. all of the above.

TRUE/FALSE QUESTIONS

1. T F   The behavioral component of an attitude refers to an intention to behave in a certain way toward someone or something.

2. T F   High rewards can act to make dissonance less important.

3. T F   Satisfaction and productivity have a high and consistent relationship.

4. T F   A combination of traits that classifies a person is called his or her attitude.

5. T F   People with an internal locus of control believe that their lives are controlled by others.

6. T F   Machiavellianism is a measure of the degree to which people are pragmatic, maintain emotional distance, and believe that ends justify means.

7. T F   We interpret what we see using our perceptions and call it reality.

8. T F   Individuals assimilate all they observe to make assessments of others.

9. T F   "Union people expect something for nothing" is an example of stereotyping.

10. T F   Operant conditioning argues that behavior is a function of its consequences.

11. T F   Managers are interested in every attitude an employee might hold.

12. T F   "Learning by mistakes" is an example of modeling.

13. T F   Cognitive dissonance is a part of social learning theory.

14. T F   People low in self-esteem are less susceptible to external influence than those people high in self-esteem.

15. T F   When people observe others, they tend to develop explanations of why they behave in certain ways.

MATCH TERMS WITH DEFINITIONS

a. Shaping behavior
b. Social learning theory
c. Operant conditioning
d. Self-serving bias
e. Perception
f. Cognitive component of an attitude
g. Affective component of an attitude
h. Cognitive dissonance
i. Attitudes
j. Stereotyping
k. Fundamental attribution error
l. Authoritarianism
m. Machiavellianism
n. Halo effect
o. Self-monitoring
p. Attribution theory
q. Learning
r. Organizational behavior

___ 1. The beliefs, opinions, knowledge, or information held by a person.

___ 2. The tendency for individuals to attribute their own successes to internal factors while putting the blame for failures on external factors.

___ 3. The process of organizing and interpreting sensory impressions in order to give meaning to the environment.

___ 4. Any incompatibility between two or more attitudes or between behavior and attitudes.

___ 5. A measure of a person's belief that there should be status and power differences among people in organizations.

___ 6. A measure of the degree to which people are pragmatic, maintain emotional distance, and believe that ends can justify means.

___ 7. The emotional or feeling segment of an attitude.

___ 8. A general impression of an individual based on a single characteristic.

___ 9. The tendency to underestimate the influence of external factors and overestimate the influence of internal factors when making judgments about the behavior of others.

___ 10. The study of the actions of people at work.

___ 11. A personality trait that measures an individual's ability to adjust his or her behavior to external situational factors.

___ 12. Any relatively permanent change in behavior that occurs as a result of experience.

___ 13. A theory used to develop explanations of how we judge people differently depending on the meaning we attribute to a given behavior.

___ 14. Evaluative statements concerning objects, people, or events.

___ 15. Judging a person on the basis of one's perception of a group to which he or she belongs.

___ 16. A type of conditioning in which desired voluntary behavior leads to a reward or prevents a punishment.

___ 17. People can learn through observation and direct experience.

___ 18. Systematically reinforcing each successive step that moves an individual closer to the desired response.

CHAPTER 14

UNDERSTANDING GROUPS AND TEAMS

Chapter Objectives

1. Contrast formal and informal groups.
2. Explain why people join groups.
3. Describe the five stages of group development.
4. Identify how roles and norms influence an employee's behavior.
5. Describe the key components in the group behavior model.
6. Explain the increased popularity of teams in organizations.
7. Describe the different types of teams found in organizations.
8. List the characteristics of effective teams.
9. Identify how managers can build trust.
10. Describe what activities are associated with managing teams.
11. Explain the role of teams in TQM.

Chapter Outline

I. Understanding Group Behavior

    A. What is a Group?

        1. Formal groups

        2. Informal groups

    B. Stages of Group Development

C. Basic Group Concepts

    1. Roles

    2. Norms and Conformity

    3. Status Systems

    4. Group Size

    5. Group Cohesiveness

D. Toward Understanding Work Group Behavior

    1. External Conditions Imposed on the Group

    2. Group Member Resources

    3. Group Structure

    4. Group Processes

    5. Group Tasks

II. Turning Groups Into Effective Teams

  A. What is a Team?

  B. Types of Teams.

  C. Why Use Teams?

    1. Creates Esprit de Corps

    2. Allows Management to Think Strategically

    3. Speeds Decisions

    4. Facilitates Workforce Diversity

    5. Increases Performance

III. Developing and Managing Effective Teams

  A. Characteristics of Effective Teams

    1. Clear Goals

    2. Relevant Skills

        3. Mutual Trust

        4. Unified Commitment

        5. Good Communication

        6. Negotiating Skills

        7. Appropriate Leadership

        8. Internal and External Support

  B. Managing Teams

        1. Planning

        2. Organizing

        3. Leading

        4. Controlling

  C. Teams and TQM

Key Terms

Group - Two or more interacting and interdependent individuals who come together to achieve particular objectives.

    Forming - The first stage in group development during which people join the group and then define the group's purpose, structure, and leadership; characterized by uncertainty.

    Storming - The second stage of group development characterized by intragroup conflict.

    Norming - The third stage of group development, characterized by close relationships and cohesiveness.

    Performing - The fourth stage in group development when the group is fully functional.

    Adjourning - The final stage in group development for temporary groups, characterized by concern with wrapping up activities rather than task performance.

Role - A set of behavior patterns expected of someone occupying a given position in a social unit.

Norms - Acceptable standards shared by a group's members.

Status - A prestige grading, position, or rank within a group.

Free rider tendency - The reduction of effort that individual members contribute to the group as it increases in size.

Group cohesiveness - The degree to which members are attracted to one another and share the group's goals.

Work teams - Formal groups made up of interdependent individuals, responsible for attaining a goal.

> **Functional team** - A type of work team that's composed of a manager and his or her subordinates from a particular functional area.
>
> **Self-directed or self-managed team** - A type of work team that operates without a manager and is responsible for a complete work process or segment that delivers a product or service to an external or internal customer.
>
> **Cross-functional team** - A type of work team in which a hybrid grouping of individuals who are experts in various specialties (or functions) work together on various organizational tasks.

Gainsharing - A group incentive program that shares the gains of the efforts of group members with those group members.

Quality Circles - Work groups that meet regularly to discuss, investigate, and correct quality problems.

MULTIPLE CHOICE QUESTIONS

1. The group development stage when close relationships develop is called

    a. performing.
    b. norming.
    c. storming.
    d. forming.

2. Group energy is focused on performing the task in the _____ stage of the group development model.

   a. performing.
   b. norming.
   c. storming.
   d. forming.

3. Intragroup conflict is high in the _____ stage of the group development model.

   a. performing.
   b. norming.
   c. storming.
   d. forming.

4. The _____ stage of the group development model is complete when members have begun to think of themselves as part of a group.

   a. performing.
   b. norming.
   c. storming.
   d. forming.

5. The _____ stage of group development is complete when a relatively clear hierarchy of leadership is recognized in the group.

   a. performing.
   b. norming.
   c. storming.
   d. forming.

6. _____ dictate(s) output levels, absenteeism rates, and promptness or tardiness.

   a. Status
   b. Norms
   c. Group cohesiveness
   d. Roles

7. A set of expected behavior patterns attributed to someone who occupies a given position in an organization can be called

   a. status.
   b. norms.
   c. group cohesiveness.
   d. roles.

8. _____ can be informally conferred on individuals because of their education, age, sex skill, or experience.

   a. Status
   b. Norms
   c. Group cohesiveness
   d. Roles

9. Which is not true for work group behavior?

   a. A group's potential level of performance depends to a large extent on the resources that its members individually bring to the group.
   b. Work groups have a structure that shapes members' behavior.
   c. Attributes that tend to have a positive connotation in our culture tend to be positively related to group productivity and morale.
   d. Effective communication and minimal levels of conflict should be more relevant to group performance when one group's tasks are independent of other unit work units' tasks.

10. Which statement is true for teams?

    a. All teams must be supervised.
    b. All teams are formed around functional tasks.
    c. Functional department teams that are part of the formal structure are permanent.
    d. All of the above.

11. Mary is part of a team which is a formal group who has no manager and is responsible for a complete work process. What kind of group is it?

    a. functional team
    b. cross-functional team.
    c. self-directed team.
    d. task force

12. Teams are popular in industry currently because

    a. they create esprit de corps.
    b. allow management to think strategically.
    c. facilitate workforce diversity.
    d. all of the above.

13. Effective teams have the following characteristic(s).

    a. clear goals.
    b. relevant skills.
    c. unified commitment.
    d. all of the above.

14. A typical Quality Circle

    a. suggest solutions and then analyzes the situation to see if there is a problem.
    b. contains about 10 to 15 members from different departments.
    c. makes the final decision for any solution they generate.
    d. assumes responsibility for solving quality problems.

15. Gainsharing is

    a. an individual performance reward system.
    b. an incentive program that shares gains of company with top managers.
    c. an insurance program for employees.
    d. an incentive program that relates rewards directly to performance.

16. The external conditions imposed from outside onto groups include

    a. organization's overall strategy
    b. general physical layout of the work space
    c. authority structures
    d. all of the above

17. When managing a team, the basic functions of management should be considered. Which of the following is not one of those functions?

    a. leading
    b. performing
    c. planning
    d. organizing

18. In the example about Ford's introduction of quality problem-solving teams, the company's management identified goals. Which of the following is not one of those goals?

    a. large enough to be efficient
    b. properly train members
    c. allocate enough time to work on problems
    d. delegate enough authority for the team to implement corrective action

19. Managers can build trust by

    a. communicating openly.
    b. being respectful.
    c. demonstrating competence.
    d. all of the above.

20. The group behavior model explains a group's satisfaction with all but one of the following

   a. internal processes within the group aid performance.
   b. a high level of independence from the larger organization.
   c. a group structure shapes behavior of members.
   d. the task the group is doing.

TRUE/FALSE QUESTIONS

1. T F   Most people join a group because of needs for security, status, self-esteem, affiliation, power, and goal achievement.

2. T F   Storming is a stage of group development characterized by close relationships and cohesiveness.

3. T F   Groups proceed through the five stages of group development, in order beginning with forming and ending with adjourning.

4. T F   If cohesiveness is low and goals are supported, productivity increases but not as much as when both cohesiveness and goal support are high.

5. T F   Every work group is influence by external conditions imposed from outside the work group.

6. T F   The structural variables that shape group members' behavior include roles, norms, and formal leadership.

7. T F   A task force is a permanent group created to maintain a function.

8. T F   A command group is determined by formal authority relationships and pictured on the organization chart.

9. T F   Even though each group has its own set of norms, there are common classes of norms that appear in most organizations.

10. T F   In his study of group conformity, Asch found that there is pressure in a group for individuals to conform to the group norm.

11. T F   When the results of a group cannot be attributed to any single person, the relationship between an individual input and the group's output is difficult to determine.

12. T F   When organizations use work teams, managers have less time for strategic planning because they are busy coordinating the efforts of the work groups.

13. T F   The more cohesive a group is, the more its members will follow its goals.

14. T F   The introduction of teams to the workplace does not automatically increase the organizations's productivity.

15. T F   Process factors (gains and losses) are critical to understanding work group behavior.

MATCH TERMS WITH DEFINITIONS

a. Group cohesiveness
b. Gainsharing
c. Forming
d. Norming
e. Storming
f. Quality Circles
g. Cross-functional teams
h. Self-directed or self-managed team
i. Functional team
j. Work teams
k. Adjourning
l. Status
m. Free rider tendency
n. Norms
o. Performing
p. Role
q. Group

___ 1. The degree to which members are attracted to one another and share the group's goals.

___ 2. Formal groups made up of interdependent individuals, responsible for attaining a goal.

___ 3. The second stage of group development characterized by intragroup conflict.

___ 4. A set of behavior patterns expected of someone occupying a given position in a social unit.

___ 5. The fourth stage in group development when the group is fully functional.

___ 6. The final stage in group development for temporary groups, characterized by concern with wrapping up activities rather than task performance.

___ 7. A prestige grading, position, or rank within a group.

___ 8. The reduction of effort that individual members contribute to the group as it increases in size.

___ 9. Two or more interacting and interdependent individuals who come together to achieve particular objectives.

___ 10. Acceptable standards shared by a group's members.

___ 11. A type of work team that's composed of a manager and his or her subordinates from a particular functional area.

___ 12. The first stage in group development during which people join the group and then define the group's purpose, structure, and leadership; characterized by uncertainty.

___ 13. The third stage of group development, characterized by close relationships and cohesiveness.

___ 14. A type of work team that operates without a manager and is responsible for a complete work process or segment that delivers a product or service to an external or internal customer.

___ 15. A type of work team in which a hybrid grouping of individuals who are experts in various specialties (or functions) work together on various organizational tasks.

___ 16. A group incentive program that shares the gains of the efforts of group members with those group members.

___ 17. Work groups that meet regularly to discuss, investigate, and correct quality problems.

CHAPTER 15

MOTIVATING EMPLOYEES

Chapter Objectives

1. Describe the motivation process.

2. Explain the hierarchy of needs theory.

3. Differentiate Theory X from Theory Y.

4. Explain the motivational implications of the motivation-hygiene theory.

5. Identify the characteristics that high achievers seek in a job.

6. Explain how goals motivate people.

7. Differentiate reinforcement theory from goal-setting theory.

8. Describe ways to design motivating jobs.

9. Describe the motivational implications of equity theory.

10. Explain the key relationships in expectancy theory.

11. Identify management practices that are likely to lead to more motivated employees.

Chapter Outline

I. What is Motivation?

II. Early Theories of Motivation

    A. Hierarchy of Needs Theory

        1. Physiological Needs

        2. Safety Needs

        3. Social Needs

        4. Esteem Needs

        5. Self-Actualization Needs

    B. Theory X and Theory Y

    C. Motivation-Hygiene Theory

III. Contemporary Approaches to Motivation

    A. Three-Needs Theory

        1. Need for Achievement

        2. Need for Power

        3. Need for Affiliation

    B. Goal-Setting Theory

    C. Reinforcement Theory

    D. Designing Motivating Jobs

        1. Job Enlargement

        2. Job Enrichment

        3. Job Characteristics Model

            a. Skill variety

            b. Task identity

            c. Task significance

            d. Autonomy

            e. Feedback

    E. Equity Theory

    F. Expectancy Theory

        1. Expectancy

        2. Instrumentality

        3. Valence

    G. Integrating Contemporary Theories of Motivation

IV. Contemporary Issues in Motivation

    A. Motivating a Diverse Workforce

    B. Pay for Performance

    C. Employee Stock Ownership Plans (ESOPs)

    D. Motivating Minimum-Wage Employees

V. From Theory to Practice: Suggestions for Motivating Employees

    A. Recognize Individual Differences

    B. Match people to Jobs

    C. Use Goals

    D. Ensure That Goals are Perceived as Attainable

    E. Individualize Rewards

    F. Link Rewards to Performance

    G. Check the System for Equity

    H. Don't Ignore Money

Key Terms

Motivation - The willingness to exert high levels of effort to reach organizational goals, conditioned by the effort's ability to satisfy some individual need.

Need - An internal state that makes certain outcomes appear attractive.

Hierarchy of needs theory - Maslow's theory that there's a hierarchy of five human needs: physiological, safety, social esteem, and self actualization. As each need is substantially satisfied, the next becomes dominant.

    Physiological needs - Basic food, drink, shelter, and sexual needs.

    Safety needs - A person's needs for security and protection from physical and emotional harm.

Social needs - A person's needs for affection, belongingness, acceptance, and friendship.

Esteem needs - Internal factors such as self-respect, autonomy, and achievement; and external factors such as status, recognition, and attention.

Self-actualization needs - A person's drive to become what he or she is capable of becoming.

Theory X - The assumption that employees dislike work, are lazy, seek to avoid responsibility, and must be coerced to perform.

Theory Y - The assumption that employees are creative, seek responsibility, and can exercise self-direction.

Motivation-hygiene theory - The theory that intrinsic factors are related to job satisfaction, while extrinsic factors are associated with dissatisfaction.

Hygiene factors - Factors that eliminate dissatisfaction.

Motivators - Factors that increase job satisfaction.

Three-needs theory - The needs for achievement, power, and affiliation are major motives in work.

Need for achievement (nAch) - The drive to excel, to achieve in relation to a set of standards, to strive to succeed.

Need for power (nPow) - The need to make others behave in a way that they wouldn't have behaved otherwise.

Need for affiliation (nAff) - The desire for friendly and close interpersonal relationships.

Goal-setting theory - Specific goals increase performance and difficult goals, when accepted, result in higher performance than easy goals.

Reinforcement theory - Behavior is a function of its consequences.

Reinforcer - Any consequence immediately following a response that increases the probability that the behavior will be repeated.

Job design - The way tasks are combined to form complete jobs.

Job scope - The number of different tasks required in a job and the frequency with which these tasks are repeated.

Job enlargement - The horizontal expansion of a job; an increase in job scope.

Job enrichment - Vertical expansion of a job by adding planning and evaluating responsibilities.

Job depth - The degree of control employees have over their work.

Job Characteristics Model (JCM) - A framework for analyzing and designing jobs; identifies five primary job characteristics, their interrelationships, and impact on outcome variables.

Skill variety - The degree to which a job requires a variety of activities so that an employee can use a number of different skills and talents.

Task Identity - The degree to which a job requires completion of a whole and identifiable piece of work.

Task significance - The degree to which a job has a substantial impact on the lives or work of other people.

Autonomy - The degree to which a job provides substantial freedom, independence, and discretion to a person in scheduling and carrying out his or her work.

Feedback - The degree to which carrying out the work activities required by a job results in a person's obtaining direct and clear information about the effectiveness of his or her performance.

Equity theory - The theory that an employee compares his or her job's inputs-outcomes ratio to that of relevant others and then corrects any inequity.

Referents - The people, systems, or selves against which a person compares him or herself to assess equity.

Expectancy theory - The theory that an individual tends to act in a certain way based on the expectation that the act will be followed by a given outcome and on the attractiveness of that outcome to the individual.

Compressed workweek - A workweek comprised of four 10-hour days.

Flexible work hours (flextime) - A scheduling system in which employees are required to work a number of hours a week, but are free within limits, to vary the hours of work.

Job sharing - The practice of having two or more people split a forty-hour-a-week job.

Telecommuting - The linking by computer and modem of workers at home with co-workers and management at an office.

Pay-for-performance - Compensation plans that pay employees on the basis of some performance measure.

Employee stock ownership plan (ESOP) - A compensation program in which employees become part owners of the organization by receiving stock as a performance incentive.

MULTIPLE CHOICE QUESTIONS

1. Which theory was developed by Douglas McGregor?

    a. hierarchy of needs theory
    b. theory of X and theory of Y
    c. motivation-hygiene theory
    d. three-needs theory

2. Which theory was developed by Frederick Herzberg?

    a. hierarchy of needs theory
    b. theory of X and theory of Y
    c. motivation-hygiene theory
    d. three-needs theory

3. Which of the following explains differences in employee motivation levels?

    a. differences in goals.
    b. differences in expectations.
    c. differences in reinforcement.
    d. all of the above

4. In expectancy theory, an individual's perception that exerting a given amount of effort will result in successful performance of a job is an example of

    a. attractiveness.
    b. referent.
    c. performance-reward linkage.
    d. effort-performance linkage.

5. A higher order need that is satisfied when a person is recognized by the boss for doing a good job is

    a. safety.
    b. social.
    c. esteem.
    d. self-actualization.

6. Theory Y managers assume that

    a. physiological and social needs dominate the individual.
    b. lower-order needs dominate the individual.
    c. higher-order needs dominate the individual.
    d. none of the above.

7. When discussing satisfaction, workers in the Herzberg study mentioned

    a. company policy.
    b. working conditions.
    c. supervision.
    d. responsibility and advancement.

8. Individuals with a high need for _____ prefer cooperative situations and desire relationships involving a high degree of mutual understanding.

    a. achievement.
    b. affiliation.
    c. power.
    d. all of the above.

9. A large Wall Street law firm that requires new associates to work for many different partners before choosing an area of specialization is an example of

    a. job specialization.
    b. job rotation.
    c. job enlargement.
    d. job enrichment.

10. The use of _____ increases job scope.

    a. job specialization.
    b. job rotation.
    c. job enlargement.
    d. job enrichment.

11. The use of _____ increases job depth.

    a. job specialization.
    b. job rotation.
    c. job enlargement.
    d. job enrichment.

12. A production worker, who in the past has done one specific activity, now does three different activities that require the same kinds of skills:

    a. job specialization.
    b. job rotation.
    c. job enlargement.
    d. job enrichment.

13. A negative effect of _____ is that production can suffer because of training needs. A worker is moved to a new job just as they become efficient at the present one.

    a. job specialization.
    b. job rotation.
    c. job enlargement.
    d. job enrichment.

14. _____ describes the job design used when a worker has one simple, repetitive job on an assembly line.

    a. job specialization.
    b. job rotation.
    c. job enlargement.
    d. job enrichment.

15. A maintenance worker at a nuclear power plant recognizes that her job is important to society at large. She is an example of which core dimension of the job characteristics model?

    a. skill variety
    b. task identity
    c. task significance
    d. autonomy

16. A worker does not relate to _____, a core dimension of the job characteristics model because he does not use different skills and talents in his job.

    a. skill variety
    b. task identity
    c. task significance
    d. autonomy

17. A worker who schedules her own work and decides how to approach her job, has a feeling of

    a. skill variety.
    b. task identity.
    c. task significance.
    d. autonomy.

18. A worker with a specialized job and little vision of the importance of his job to the finished product would not identify with the core dimension of _____.

    a. skill variety.
    b. task identity.
    c. task significance.
    d. autonomy.

19. When full-time production employees work 4 10-hour days each week, their company is using _____.

    a. compressed workweek.
    b. flextime.
    c. job sharing.
    d. telecommuting.

20. A full-time employee must work in the office from 9:00am to 11:00am each day but can schedule the rest of her work time to match her needs. This employee works for a company which uses _____.

    a. compressed workweek.
    b. flextime.
    c. job sharing.
    d. telecommuting.

TRUE/FALSE QUESTION

1. T F   Motivation is the result of the interaction between the individual and the situation.

2. T F   According to the hierarchy of needs theory, a substantially satisfied need no longer motivates.

3. T F   Physiological, safety, and social needs are described as lower-order needs.

4. T F   Theory X is the assumption that employees are creative, seek responsibility, and can exercise self-direction.

5. T F   In Herzberg's motivation-hygiene theory, intrinsic factors such as recognition, the work itself, responsibility, and advancement were found to be related to job satisfaction.

6. T F   According to Herzberg, eliminating dissatisfaction does not necessarily lead to motivation and job satisfaction.

7. T F   Reinforcement theory ignores the inner state of the individual and concentrates solely on what happens to a person when she/he takes some action.

8. T F   In equity theory, individuals are concerned only with the absolute rewards they receive for their efforts.

9. T F   Expectancy theory is a contingency approach to motivation.

10. T F   According to expectancy theory, money is not a motivator.

11. T F   Even though employees have different needs, reinforcers are the same for all employees.

12. T F   Job enrichment is horizontal expansion of a job by increasing job scope.

13. T F   Job specialization is synonymous with division of labor.

14. T F   Task significance, one of the core dimensions in the job characteristics model, is the degree to which a job requires completion of a whole and identifiable piece of work.

15. T F   Flextime tends to reduce absenteeism, make planning an control easier, and is less expensive for organizations.

MATCH TERMS WITH DEFINITIONS

a. Hierarchy of needs theory
b. Equity theory
c. Task Identity
d. Reinforcement theory
e. Task significance
f. Job Characteristics Model
g. Job depth
h. Theory Y
i. Theory X
j. Motivators
k. Goal-setting theory
l. Skill variety
m. Job scope
n. Need for power (nPow)
o. Need for achievement (nAch)
p. Need for affiliation (nAff)
q. Job enrichment
r. Hygiene factors
s. Motivation
t. Expectancy theory

___ 1. Behavior is a function of its consequences.

___ 2. The assumption that employees are creative, seek responsibility, and can exercise self-direction.

___ 3. Specific goals increase performance and difficult goals, when accepted, result in higher performance than easy goals.

___ 4. The assumption that employees dislike work, are lazy, seek to avoid responsibility, and must be coerced to perform.

___ 5. Factors that increase job satisfaction.

___ 6. The theory that an individual tends to act in a certain way based on the expectation that the act will be followed by a given outcome and on the attractiveness of that outcome to the individual.

___ 7. The drive to excel, to achieve in relation to a set of standards, to strive to succeed.

___ 8. The willingness to exert high levels of effort to reach organizational goals, conditioned by the effort's ability to satisfy some individual need.

___ 9. The desire for friendly and close interpersonal relationships.

___ 10. Vertical expansion of a job by adding planning and evaluating responsibilities.

___ 11. The need to make others behave in a way that they wouldn't have behaved otherwise.

___ 12. The number of different tasks required in a job and the frequency with which these tasks are repeated.

___ 13. The degree to which a job requires a variety of activities so that an employee can use a number of different skills and talents.

___ 14. The degree of control employees have over their work.

___ 15. A framework for analyzing and designing jobs; identifies five primary job characteristics, their interrelationships, and impact on outcome variables.

___ 16. Factors that eliminate dissatisfaction.

___ 17. The degree to which a job has a substantial impact on the lives or work of other people.

___ 18. The theory that an employee compares his or her job's inputs-outcomes ratio to that of relevant others and then corrects any inequity.

___ 19. Maslow's theory that there's a hierarchy of five human needs: physiological, safety, social esteem, and self actualization. As each need is substantially satisfied, the next becomes dominant.

___ 20. The degree to which a job requires completion of a whole and identifiable piece of work.

CHAPTER 16

LEADERSHIP

Chapter Objectives

1. Explain the difference between managers and leaders.

2. Summarize the conclusions of trait theories.

3. Describe the various behavioral styles that leaders use.

4. Identify the two underlying leadership behaviors and the five key leadership styles in the managerial grid.

5. Describe the Fiedler contingency model.

6. Explain the Hersey-Blanchard situational theory.

7. Summarize the path-goal model.

8. Explain the attribution theory of leadership.

9. Describe the key characteristics of charismatic leaders.

10. Contrast transactional and transformational leadership.

11. Identify the various sources of power a leader might possess.

12. Explain gender and cultural differences in leadership.

13. Explain when leaders might not be that important.

Chapter Outline

I. Managers Versus Leaders

II. Trait Theories

III. Behavioral Theories

    A. Autocratic-Democratic Continuum

    B. The Ohio State Studies

    C. The University of Michigan Studies

    D. The Managerial Grid

    E. Summary of Behavioral Theories

IV. Contingency Theories

    A. The Fiedler Model

    B. The Hersey-Blanchard Situational Theory

    C. Path-Goal Theory

    D. Leader Participation Model

    E. Summary of Contingency Theories

V. Emerging Approaches to Leadership

    A. Attribution Theory of Leadership

    B. Charismatic Leadership Theory

VI. Contemporary Issues in Leadership

    A. Leaders and Power

        1. Legitimate Power

        2. Coercive Power

        3. Reward Power

        4. Expert Power

        5. Referent Power

    B. Leading Through Empowerment

    C. Gender and Leadership

        1. The Evidence

        2. Is Different Better?

        3. A Few Concluding Thoughts

    D. Leadership Styles and Different Cultures

    E. Sometimes Leadership Is Irrelevant!

Key Terms

Leaders - those who are able to influence others and who possess managerial authority.

Trait theories - theories isolating characteristics that differentiate leaders from nonleaders.

Behavioral theories - Theories identifying behaviors that differentiate effective from ineffective leaders.

Autocratic style - Describes a leader who typically tends to centralize authority, dictate work methods, make unilateral decisions, and limit subordinate participation.

Democratic style - Describes a leader who tends to involve subordinates in decision making, delegate authority, encourage participation in deciding work methods and goals, and use feedback as an opportunity for coaching.

Laissez-faire style - Describes a leader who generally gives the group complete freedom to make decisions and complete the work in whatever way it sees fit.

Initiating structure - The extent to which a leader defines and structures his or her role and those of subordinates to attain goals.

Consideration - The extent to which a person has job relationships characterized by mutual trust, respect for subordinates' ideas, and regard for their feelings.

High-high leader - A leader high in both initiating structure and consideration.

Managerial grid - A two-dimensional portrayal of leadership based on concerns for people and for production.

Fiedler contingency model - The theory that effective groups depend on a proper match between a leader's style of interacting with subordinates and the degree to which the situation gives control and influence to the leader.

> **Least-preferred co-worker (LPC) questionnaire** - A questionnaire that measures whether a person is task or relationship oriented.
>
> **Leader-member relations** - The degree of confidence, trust, and respect subordinates have in their leader.
>
> **Task structure** - The degree to which the job assignments are procedurized.
>
> **Position power** - The degree of influence a leader has over power variables such as hiring, firing, discipline, promotions, and salary increases.

Situational leadership theory - A contingency theory that focuses on followers' maturity.

Readiness - The ability and willingness of people to take responsibility for directing their own behavior.

Path-goal theory - The theory that a leader's behavior is acceptable to subordinates insofar as they view it as a source of either immediate or future satisfaction.

Leader participation model - A leadership theory that provides a set of rules to determine the form and amount of participative decision making in different situations.

Attribution theory of leadership - Proposes that leadership is merely an attribution that people make about other individuals.

Charismatic leadership - Followers make attributions of heroic or extraordinary leadership abilities when they observe certain behaviors.

Transactional leaders - Leaders who guide or motivate their followers in the direction of established goals by clarifying role and task requirements.

Transformational leaders - Leader who provide individualized consideration, intellectual stimulation, and possess charisma.

Sources of Power

> **Legitimate power** - The power a person has as a result of his or her position in the formal organizational hierarchy; also called 'authority'.
>
> **Coercive power** - Power that rests on the application, or the threat of application, of physical sanctions such as the infliction of pain; the arousal of frustration through restriction of movement; or the controlling force of basic physiological or safety needs.
>
> **Reward power** - Power that produces positive benefits or rewards.

Expert power - Influence that results from expertise, special skill, or knowledge.

Referent power - Power that arises from identification with a person who has desirable resources or personal traits.

MULTIPLE CHOICE QUESTIONS

1. Theories isolating characteristics that differentiate leaders from nonleaders are

    a. behavioral theories
    b. trait theories
    c. contingency theories
    d. none of the above

2. Theories identifying situational influences on leader effectiveness are

    a. behavioral theories
    b. trait theories
    c. contingency theories
    d. none of the above

3. "Leaders are born and not made" illustrates

    a. behavioral theories
    b. trait theories
    c. contingency theories
    d. none of the above

4. Which of the following is a contingency model of leadership?

    a. University of Michigan Studies
    b. Ohio State Studies
    c. Managerial Grid
    d. Hersey-Blanchard Model

5. Which theory uses the dimensions of initiating structure and consideration behavior?

    a. University of Michigan Studies
    b. Ohio State Studies
    c. Managerial Grid
    d. Hersey-Blanchard Model

6. This theory uses the two dimensions of employee oriented and production oriented behavior.

    a. University of Michigan Studies
    b. Ohio State Studies
    c. Managerial Grid
    d. Hersey-Blanchard Model

7. Country-club, team, and impoverished are leader styles found in this theory.

    a. University of Michigan Studies
    b. Ohio State Studies
    c. Managerial Grid
    d. Hersey-Blanchard Model

8. Results of this research suggest that leaders perform best with maximum concern for production and maximum concern for people.

    a. University of Michigan Studies
    b. Ohio State Studies
    c. Managerial Grid
    d. Hersey-Blanchard Model

9. The LPC questionnaire was used to develop situational aspects important to leaders in the following theory.

    a. Path-Goal Theory
    b. Leader-Participation Model
    c. Fiedler Contingency Model
    d. Hersey-Blanchard Situational Model

10. Maturity is an important situational factor for this theory.

    a. Path-Goal Theory
    b. Leader-Participation Model
    c. Fiedler Contingency Model
    d. Hersey-Blanchard Situational Model

11. This theory provides a sequential set of rules that should be followed in determining the form and amount of participation needed in decision making.

    a. Path-Goal Theory
    b. Leader-Participation Model
    c. Fiedler Contingency Model
    d. Hersey-Blanchard Situational Model

12. A leader's behavior is acceptable to workers insofar as they view it as a source of either immediate or future satisfaction.

    a. Path-Goal Theory
    b. Leader-Participation Model
    c. Fiedler Contingency Model
    d. Hersey-Blanchard Situational Model

13. The three situational factors in this theory are leader-member relations, task structure, and leader position power.

    a. Path-Goal Theory
    b. Leader-Participation Model
    c. Fiedler Contingency Model
    d. Hersey-Blanchard Situational Model

14. This theory proposes that leader behavior will be ineffective when it is redundant with sources of environment structure or incongruent with worker characteristics.

    a. Path-Goal Theory
    b. Leader-Participation Model
    c. Fiedler Contingency Model
    d. Hersey-Blanchard Situational Model

15. The emphasis of this theory is on characteristics of the followers, not characteristics of the leader.

    a. Path-Goal Theory
    b. Leader-Participation Model
    c. Fiedler Contingency Model
    d. Hersey-Blanchard Situational Model

16. A leader who guides or motivates followers in the direction of established goals by clarifying role and task requirements is a

    a. transactional leader.
    b. authoritative leader.
    c. transformational leader.
    d. none of the above.

17. A person who has worked in the industry for several years and is respected for her work has _____ power.

    a. coercive
    b. reward
    c. expert
    d. referent

18. A manager exercises _____ power when she allows workers to have a day off from work after completing an especially difficult project.

   a. coercive
   b. reward
   c. expert
   d. referent

19. _____ power develops out of admiration of another person and a desire to be like that person.

   a. Coercive
   b. Reward
   c. Expert
   d. Referent

20. Friendliness, acceptance, and praise illustrate _____ power which is available without legitimate authority.

   a. Coercive
   b. Reward
   c. Expert
   d. Referent

TRUE/FALSE QUESTIONS

1. T F   Manager and leader are synonymous terms.

2. T F   All managers should ideally be leaders.

3. T F   Trait theory is valid because there are specific characteristics all leaders possess.

4. T F   According to researchers, if the behavioral theory of leadership could determine critical behavior determinants of leadership, then it would be possible to train people to be leaders.

5. T F   Two popular behavioral leadership theories are the Ohio State Studies and the University of Michigan Studies.

6. T F   Two dimensions of leader behavior discussed in the Ohio State Studies were employee-oriented behavior and production-oriented behavior.

7. T F   Initiating structure from the Ohio State Studies and production oriented behavior from the University of Michigan Studies are essentially the same.

8. T F From their research findings, Blake and Mouton concluded that managers perform best using the 5,5 leader style.

9. T F The Fiedler Contingency Model proposes that effective group performance depends on the proper match between the leader's style of interacting with his/her subordinates and the degree to which the situation gives control and influence to the leader.

10. T F The Fiedler Model proposes matching an individual's LPC and an assessment of the three contingency variables to achieve maximum leadership effectiveness.

11. T F The Hersey-Blanchard Model is a behavioral theory of leadership.

13. T F Maturity is the important component in the Path-Goal Theory.

14. T F Leadership may not always be important.

15. T F Transformational leaders guide or motivate their followers in the direction of established goals by clarifying role and task requirements.

MATCH TERMS WITH DEFINITIONS

a. Consideration
b. Transformational leaders
c. Attribution theory of leadership
d. Leader participation model
e. Initiating structure
f. Task structure
g. Least-preferred co-worker (LPC)
h. Managerial grid
i. Leader-member relations
j. Position power
k. Transactional leaders
l. Path-goal theory
m. Situational leadership theory
n. Charismatic leadership
o. Leaders

___ 1. A leadership theory that provides a set of rules to determine the form and amount of participative decision making in different situations.

___ 2. The degree to which the job assignments are procedurized.

___ 3. The extent to which a leader defines and structures his or her role and those of subordinates to attain goals.

___ 4. A two-dimensional portrayal of leadership based on concerns for people and for production.

___ 5. A questionnaire that measures whether a person is task or relationship oriented.

___ 6. Those who are able to influence others and who possess managerial authority.

___ 7. The degree of confidence, trust, and respect subordinates have in their leader.

___ 8. Proposes that leadership is merely an attribution that people make about other individuals.

___ 9. The degree of influence a leader has over power variables such as hiring, firing, discipline, promotions, and salary increases.

___ 10. The extent to which a person has job relationships characterized by mutual trust, respect for subordinates' ideas, and regard for their feelings.

___ 11. Leader who provide individualized consideration, intellectual stimulation, and possess charisma.

___ 12. Followers make attributions of heroic or extraordinary leadership abilities when they observe certain behaviors.

___ 13. Leaders who guide or motivate their followers in the direction of established goals by clarifying role and task requirements.

___ 14. The theory that a leader's behavior is acceptable to subordinates insofar as they view it as a source of either immediate or future satisfaction.

___ 15. A contingency theory that focuses on followers' maturity.

CHAPTER 17

COMMUNICATION AND INTERPERSONAL SKILLS

Chapter Objectives

1. Define communication and explain why it's important to managers.
2. Describe the communication process.
3. List techniques for overcoming communication barriers.
4. Identify behaviors related to effective active listening.
5. Identify behaviors related to providing effective feedback.
6. Describe the contingency factors in delegation.
7. Identify behaviors related to effective delegating.
8. Describe the steps in analyzing and resolving conflict situations.
9. Explain when a manager might want to stimulate conflict.
10. Contrast distributive and integrative bargaining.

Chapter Outline

I. Understanding Communication

    A. What is Communication?

    B. The Communication Process

    C. Methods of Communicating

        1. Oral

        2. Written

        3. Nonverbal

        4. Electronic Media

- D. Barriers to Effective Communication
    1. Filtering
    2. Selective Perception
    3. Emotions
    4. Language
    5. National culture
    6. Nonverbal Cues
- E. Overcoming the Barriers
    1. Use Feedback
    2. Simplify Language
    3. Listen Actively
    4. Constrain Emotions
    5. Watch Nonverbal Cues

II. Developing Interpersonal Skills

- A. Active Listening Skills
    1. Active Versus Passive Listening
- B. Developing Effective Active Listening Skills
    1. Make Eye Contact
    2. Exhibit Affirmative Nods and Appropriate Facial Expressions
    3. Avoid Distracting Actions or Gestures
    4. Ask Questions
    5. Paraphrase
    6. Avoid Interrupting the Speaker
    7. Don't Overtalk
    8. Make Smooth Transitions Between the Roles of Speaker and Listener

C. Feedback Skills

    1. Positive Versus Negative Feedback

D. Developing Effective Feedback Skills

    1. Focus on Specific Behaviors

    2. Keep Feedback Impersonal

    3. Keep Feedback Goal Oriented

    4. Make Feedback Well Timed

    5. Ensure Understanding

    6. Direct Negative Feedback Toward Behavior That the Recipient Can Control

III. Delegation Skills

A. What is Delegation?

B. Is Delegation Abdication?

C. Contingency Factors in Delegation

    1. The Size of the Organization

    2. The Importance of the Duty or Decision

    3. Task Complexity

    4. Organizational Culture

    5. Qualities of Subordinates

D. Developing Effective Delegating Skills

    1. Clarify the Assignment

    2. Specify the Subordinate's Range of Discretion

    3. Allow the Subordinate to Participate

    4. Inform Others That Delegation Has Occurred

    5. Establish Feedback Channels

IV. Conflict Management Skills

    A. What is Conflict?

        1. The Traditional View

        2. The Human Relations View

        3. The Interactionist

    B. Functional Versus Dysfunctional Conflict

    C. Developing Effective Conflict Resolution Skills

        1. What is Your Preferred Conflict-Handling Style?

        2. Be Judicious in Selecting the Conflicts You Want to Handle

        3. Evaluate the Conflict Players

        4. Assess the Source of the Conflict

        5. Know Your Options

    D. What About Conflict Stimulation

        1. Change the Organization's Culture

        2. Use Communication

        3. Bring in Outsiders

        4. Restructure the Organization

        5. Appoint a "Devil's Advocate"

V. Negotiation Skills

    A. Bargaining Strategies

        1. Distributive Bargaining

        2. Integrative Bargaining

    B. Decision-Making Biases That Hinder Effective Negotiations

        1. Irrational Escalation of Commitment

        2. The Mythical Fixed Pie

       3. Anchoring Adjustments

       4. Framing Negotiations

       5. Availability of Information

       6. The Winner's Curse

       7. Overconfidence

   C. Developing Effective Negotiation Skills

       1. Research Your Opponent

       2. Begin with a Positive Overture

       3. Address Problems, Not Personalities

       4. Pay Little Attention to Initial Offers

       5. Emphasize Win-Win Solutions

       6. Be Open to Accepting Third-Party Assistance

<u>Key Terms</u>

Communication - The transferring and understanding of meaning.

Interpersonal communication - Communication between two or more people in which the parties are treated as individuals rather than objects.

Communication process - The seven stages in which meaning is transmitted and understood.

   Message - A purpose to be conveyed.

   Encoding - Converting a message into symbols.

   Channel - the medium by which a message travels.

   Decoding - Retranslating a sender's message.

   Noise - Disturbances that interfere with the transmission of a message.

Nonverbal communication - Communication transmitted without words.

Body language - Gestures, facial configurations, and other movements of the body that convey meaning.

Verbal intonation - An emphasis given to words or phrases that conveys meaning.

Electronic mail(e-mail) - Instantaneous transmission of written messages on computers that are linked together.

Filtering - The deliberate manipulation of information to make it appear more favorable to the receiver.

Active listening - Listening for full meaning without making premature judgments or interpretations.

Paraphrasing - Restating what a speaker has said but in your own words.

Delegation - The assignment of authority to another person to carry out specific activities.

Conflict - Perceived incompatible differences that result in interference or opposition.

Traditional view of conflict - The view that conflict is a natural and inevitable outcome in any organization.

Interactionist view of conflict - The view that some conflict is necessary for an organization to perform effectively.

Functional conflicts - Conflicts that support an organization's goals.

Dysfunctional conflicts - Conflicts that prevent an organization from achieving its goals.

Avoidance - Withdrawal from or suppression of conflict.

Accommodation - Resolving conflicts by placing another's needs and concerns above one's own.

Forcing - Satisfying one's own needs at the expense of another's.

Compromise - A solution to conflict in which each party gives up something of value.

Collaboration - Resolving conflict by seeking a solution advantageous to all parties.

Devil's advocate - A person who purposely presents arguments that run counter to those proposed by the majority.

Negotiation - A process in which two or more parties exchange goods or services and attempt to agree on the exchange rate for them.

> **Distributive bargaining** - Negotiations that seek to divide up a fixed amount of resources: a win-lose situation.

Integrative bargaining - Negotiation that seeks one or more settlements that can create a win-win situation.

MULTIPLE CHOICE QUESTIONS

1. When a manager writes a memo to an employee about a new company policy, she is using the _____ part of the communication process.

    a. message
    b. encoding
    c. channel
    d. noise

2. If the sender perceives that certain information is important and spends much time deciding just how the information should be communicated, they are using the _____ part of the communication process.

    a. message
    b. encoding
    c. channel
    d. noise

3. An example of the _____ part of the communication process is a manager telling a worker "You're fired!".

    a. message
    b. encoding
    c. channel
    d. noise

4. Making sure that a message has been understood is

    a. feedback
    b. noise
    c. channel
    d. decoding

5. Which is a disadvantage of written communication?

    a. The more people involved, the more likely there is to be distortion in the message.
    b. There is no built-in feedback mechanism.
    c. It is less time consuming than other methods of communication.
    d. None of the above.

6. Body language is

    a. gestures.
    b. facial configurations.
    c. movements of the body.
    d. all of the above.

7. Nonverbal communication is

    a. gestures.
    b. facial configurations and other body movements.
    c. emphasis on words and phrases.
    d. all of the above.

8. Every oral communication also has

    a. nonverbal communication.
    b. filtering.
    c. active listening.
    d. conflict.

9. A barrier to communication when a receiver sees and hears communication depending on their own needs, motivations, experiences, and other personal characteristics is called

    a. emotions.
    b. language.
    c. selective perception.
    d. filtering.

10. Deliberate manipulation of information to make it appeal more favorable to the receiver is called

    a. emotions.
    b. language.
    c. selective perception.
    d. filtering.

11. Which of the following is not a requirement for active listening?

    a. empathy
    b. acceptance and willingness to take responsibility for completeness
    c. manager keeps control in the discussion
    d. intensity

12. Which of the following is not true for paraphrasing in active listening?

    a. Paraphrasing is not important for good active listening.
    b. Paraphrasing is a control device used by a listener to be sure they have been listening carefully.
    c. Paraphrasing is a feedback mechanism.
    d. Paraphrasing is a control device a listener uses to be sure they are listening accurately.

13. Conflict stimulation is needed when

    a. the manager is surrounded by workers who are willing to express their views.
    b. new ideas are presented at every meeting.
    c. there is an excessive concern to avoid hurting members' feelings.
    d. change is accepted by subordinates.

14. Decision-making biases that can hinder effective negotiation include

    a. an irrational escalation of commitment.
    b. bargainers assume gain can only come at the expense of others.
    c. overconfidence in their own ability.
    d. all of the above.

15. The interactionist view of conflict states that

    a. all conflict is bad and must be avoided.
    b. some conflict is necessary for the organization to perform effectively.
    c. conflict is a natural and inevitable outcome in any organization.
    d. the view that conflict should support an organization's goals.

16. Resolving conflict by placing another's needs and concerns above ones's own is

    a. collaboration.
    b. accommodation.
    c. compromise.
    d. avoidance.

17. A method for resolving conflict that requires each person to give up something is

    a. collaboration.
    b. accommodation.
    c. compromise.
    d. avoidance.

18. Resolving conflict by withdrawing from the conflict is called

   a. collaboration.
   b. accommodation.
   c. compromise.
   d. avoidance.

19. When two parties have interests that are convergent or congruent, they are involved in

   a. integrative bargaining.
   b. forcing.
   c. distributive bargaining.
   d. negotiation.

20. Delegation is

   a. abdication of responsibility.
   b. an easy, common task of managers.
   c. a way to shift authority to another person to do something specific.
   d. a mistake since it involves getting work done through others.

TRUE/FALSE QUESTIONS

1. T F   Everything a manager does involves communication.

2. T F   Communication is telling another person some information.

3. T F   A receiver, who retranslates the sender's message, is encoding.

4. T F   Noise in communication is disturbances that interfere with the transmission of the message.

5. T F   Examples of communication channels include spoken words, memos, and reports.

6. T F   The major disadvantage of oral communication is that the more people who are involved, the greater the potential for distortion.

7. T F   A major disadvantage of written communication is that there is no built in feedback mechanism.

8. T F   Nonverbal communication includes body language and verbal intonation.

9. T F   Contingency factors in delegation include company size, importance of the duty or decision, job complexity, organization culture, and skill of workers.

10. T F   Don't research your opponent in negotiation because you may become sympathetic to their views.

11. T F   Integrative bargaining builds long term relationships and makes working together easier.

12. T F   The traditional view of conflict is that conflict is a natural and inevitable outcome in any organization.

13. T F   Dysfunctional conflicts prevent an organization from achieving its goals.

14. T F   Every conflict is worth a manager's time and effort.

15. T F   Distributive bargaining is a win-win approach to negotiation.

MATCH TERMS WITH DEFINITIONS

a. Traditional view of conflict
b. Delegation
c. Integrative bargaining
d. Communication
e. Encoding
f. Noise
g. Channel
h. Message
i. Accommodation
j. Interactionist view of conflict
k. Negotiation
l. Conflict
m. Filtering
n. Active listening
o. Distributive bargaining

___ 1. The transferring and understanding of meaning.

___ 2. The view that some conflict is necessary for an organization to perform effectively.

___ 3. Converting a message into symbols.

___ 4. Disturbances that interfere with the transmission of a message.

___ 5. The deliberate manipulation of information to make it appear more favorable to the receiver.

___ 6. Listening for full meaning without making premature judgments or interpretations.

___ 7. A purpose to be conveyed.

___ 8. The assignment of authority to another person to carry out specific activities.

___ 9. Negotiations that seek to divide up a fixed amount of resources: a win-lose situation.

___ 10. Perceived incompatible differences that result in interference or opposition.

___ 11. The medium by which a message travels.

___ 12. The view that conflict is a natural and inevitable outcome in any organization.

___ 13. Resolving conflicts by placing another's needs and concerns above one's own.

___ 14. A process in which two or more parties exchange goods or services and attempt to agree on the exchange rate for them.

___ 15. Negotiation that seeks one or more settlements that can create a win-win situation.

# CHAPTER 18

FOUNDATIONS OF CONTROL

Chapter Objectives

1. Define control.
2. Describe the three approaches to control.
3. Explain why control is important.
4. Describe the control process.
5. Distinguish between the three types of control.
6. Describe the qualities of an effective control system.
7. Explain how controls can become dysfunctional.
8. Identify three current ethical issues in control.

Chapter Outline

I. What is Control?

II. The Importance of Control

III. The Control Process

    A. Measuring

        1. How We Measure

        2. What We Measure

    B. Comparing

C. Taking Managerial Action

      1. Correct Actual Performance

      2. Revise the Standard

   D. Summary

IV. Types of Control

   A. Feedforward Control

   B. Concurrent Control

   C. Feedback Control

V. Qualities of an Effective Control System

   A. Effective Control System Characteristics

      1. Accuracy

      2. Timeliness

      3. Economy

      4. Flexibility

      5. Understandability

      6. Reasonable Criteria

      7. Strategic Placement

      8. Emphasis on the Exception

      9. Multiple Criteria

      10. Corrective Action

VI. Adjusting Controls for National Differences

VII. Ethical Issues in Control

   A. Employee Workplace Privacy

   B. Computer Monitoring

   C. Off-the-Job Behavior

Key Terms

Control - The process of monitoring activities to ensure they're being accomplished as planned and of correcting any significant deviations.

Market control - An approach to designing control systems that emphasizes the use of external market mechanisms to establish the standards used in the control system.

Bureaucratic control - An approach to designing control systems that emphasizes organizational authority and relies on administrative rules, regulations, procedures, policies, standardization of activities and other administrative mechanisms to ensure that employees exhibit appropriate behaviors and meet performance standards.

Clan control - An approach to designing control systems in which employee behaviors are regulated by the shared values, norms, traditions, rituals, beliefs, and other aspects of the organization's culture.

Control Process - The process of measuring actual performance, comparing it against a standard, and taking managerial action to correct deviations or inadequate standards.

Range of variation - The acceptable parameters of variance between actual performance and the standard.

Immediate corrective action - Correcting an activity at once in order to get performance back on track.

Basic corrective action - Determining how and why performance has deviated and correcting the source of deviation.

Feedforward control - Control that prevents anticipated problems.

Concurrent control - Control that occurs while an activity is in progress.

Feedback control - Control imposed after an action has occurred.

Management by walking around (MBWA) - A controlling technique in which the manager is out in the work area, interacting directly with employees, and exchanging information about what's going on.

MULTIPLE CHOICE QUESTIONS

1. Which is not true for control?

    a. Control is the final link in the functional chain of activities.
    b. All managers should be involved in control activities.
    c. Control is not important if plans are well conceived.
    d. Control is a process of measuring actual performance, comparing actual against a standard, and taking corrective action.

2. This method for measuring performance allows managers to pick up nonverbal cues.

    a. statistical reports
    b. personal observation
    c. written reports
    d. oral reports.

3. Having documents available for later reference is no longer a disadvantage of this method for measuring performance.

    a. statistical reports
    b. personal observation
    c. written reports
    d. oral reports.

4. Graphs, bar charts, and nonverbal displays are examples for this method of measuring performance.

    a. statistical reports
    b. personal observation
    c. written reports
    d. oral reports.

5. Which is not true for subjective measures of performance?

    a. Subjective measures have significant limitations.
    b. Subjective measures are preferable to objective measures for performance.
    c. Subjective measures are better than having no standard at all.
    d. Often subjective measures can be broken down into objective parts.

6. A manager changes the planned sales level for the work group from 10,000 to 8,000 units. This is an example of

    a. basic corrective action.
    b. do nothing.
    c. immediate corrective action.
    d. revising the standard.

7. Since salespeople are not achieving expectations, a manager cuts the price by 30% hoping to increase sales. This is an example of

   a. basic corrective action.
   b. do nothing.
   c. immediate corrective action.
   d. revising the standard.

8. A manager finds that salespeople are not achieving their quotas, but the sales are within the range of deviation. This is an example of

   a. basic corrective action.
   b. do nothing.
   c. immediate corrective action.
   d. revising the standard.

9. Since salespeople are not achieving expectations, a manager traces the problem to use of incorrect distribution channels and the manager changes the distribution channel. This is an example of

   a. basic corrective action.
   b. do nothing.
   c. immediate corrective action.
   d. revising the standard.

10. _____ is used to prevent anticipated problems.

    a. Feedforward control.
    b. Basic control.
    c. Concurrent control.
    d. Feedback control.

11. _____ occurs while an activity is in progress.

    a. Feedforward control
    b. Basic control
    c. Concurrent control
    d. Feedback control

12. _____ is imposed after an action has occurred.

    a. Feedforward control
    b. Basic control
    c. Concurrent control
    d. Feedback control

13. _____ is the most desirable type of control.

    a. Feedforward control
    b. Basic control
    c. Concurrent control
    d. Feedback control

14. The major disadvantage of _____ is that by the time managers know there is a deviation, the damage has been done.

    a. feedforward control
    b. basic control
    c. concurrent control
    d. feedback control

15. Direct supervision is an example of

    a. feedforward control.
    b. basic control.
    c. concurrent control.
    d. feedback control.

16. _____ has two advantages over the other types of control--managers have meaningful information on how effective planning was and employee motivation usually improves.

    a. Feedforward control
    b. Basic control
    c. Concurrent control
    d. Feedback control

17. What do managers control?

    a. people and information.
    b. finances
    c. operations
    d. all of the above

18. Ethical issues in control include

    a. computer monitoring of employee work performance.
    b. employee workplace email privacy.
    c. off-the-job behavior like smoking at home.
    d. all of the above.

19. Which of the following statements regarding dysfunctional controls is not true?

    a. Dysfunctional control systems are flexible.
    b. People can lose sight of organization's goals.
    c. Dysfunctionality is caused by incomplete measures of performance.
    d. Appearance rather than performance becomes the focus.

20. National differences affect controls systems because

    a. laws in some countries don't allow management to layoff employees.
    b. technology is more prevalent in some countries than others.
    c. amount of labor intensity varies.
    d. all of the above.

TRUE/FALSE QUESTIONS

1. T F   All managers should be involved in the control function even if their units are performing as planned.

2. T F   Managers can effectively carry out most control activities in the organization by personally observing the activity.

3. T F   A disadvantage of statistical reports as a method of control measurement is that these reports provide limited information about an activity.

4. T F   The performance of some activities is difficult to measure in quantifiable terms.

5. T F   Subjective measures are limited, but they are better than having no standards for control.

6. T F   Any deviation from the plan needs corrective attention.

7. T F   A manager takes basic corrective action by determining how and why the performance deviation occurred and correcting the source of the deviation.

8. T F   "Putting out fires" describes the basic corrective action approach to control.

9. T F   Feedback controls are desirable because they allow management to prevent problems rather than cure them later.

10. T F   Direct supervision is the best known form of concurrent control.

11. T F   Feedforward control provides information that will help employees know how well they have performed.

12. T F   An effective control system not only indicates when a significant deviation from standard occurs, but also suggest what action should be taken to correct the deviation.

13. T F   The greater the degree of decentralization, the more managers need feedback on the performance of subordinates' decision making.

14. T F   Extensive controls are likely to be implemented if an error would be highly damaging to the organization.

15. T F   Employees may resort to unethical or illegal shortcuts to meet organizational standards.

MATCH TERMS WITH DEFINITIONS

a. Range of variation
b. Basic corrective action
c. Concurrent control
d. Control process
e. Immediate corrective action
f. Feedforward control
g. Feedback control
h. Control
i. Market control
j. Bureaucratic control
k. Clan control
l. Management by walking around (MBWA)

___ 1. Correcting an activity at once in order to get performance back on track.

___ 2. An approach to designing control systems that emphasizes the use of external market mechanisms to establish the standards used in the control system.

___ 3. A controlling technique in which the manager is out in the work area, interacting directly with employees, and exchanging information about what's going on.

___ 4. An approach to designing control systems in which employee behaviors are regulated by the shared values, norms, traditions, rituals, beliefs, and other aspects of the organization's culture.

___ 5. Control that occurs while an activity is in progress.

___ 6. The process of measuring actual performance, comparing it against a standard, and taking managerial action to correct deviations or inadequate standards.

___ 7. The acceptable parameters of variance between actual performance and the standard.

___ 8. The process of monitoring activities to ensure they're being accomplished as planned and of correcting any significant deviations.

___ 9. Determining how and why performance has deviated and correcting the source of deviation.

___ 10. Control imposed after an action has occurred.

___ 11. An approach to designing control systems that emphasizes organizational authority and relies on administrative rules, regulations, procedures, policies, standardization of activities and other administrative mechanisms to ensure that employees exhibit appropriate behaviors and meet performance standards.

___ 12. Control that prevents anticipated problems.

CHAPTER 19

OPERATIONS MANAGEMENT

Chapter Objectives

1. Describe the role of the transformation process in operations management.

2. Explain what factors determine organizational productivity.

3. Discuss what re-engineering of work processes involves.

4. Describe how adding a "manufacturing focus" to organizational strategy affects an organization.

5. Identify the four key decisions that provide the long-term strategic direction for operations planning.

6. Describe the three decisions that make up tactical operations planning.

7. Identify the three approaches to maintenance control.

8. Explain the contingency factors that affect the implementation of TQM.

9. Discuss the advantages and potential problems of just-in-time (JIT) inventory systems.

10. Explain how flexible manufacturing systems could give an organization a competitive advantage.

11. Describe how speed can be a competitive advantage.

Chapter Outline

I. Operations Management and the Transformation Process

II. Managing Productivity

   A. Deming's Fourteen Points

III. Operations Management Includes Both Manufacturing and Services

IV. Re-engineering Work Processes

V. Strategic Operations Management

VI. Planning Operations

    A. Capacity Planning

    B. Facilities Location Planning

    C. Process Planning

    D. Facilities Layout Planning

    E. Aggregate Planning

    F. Master Scheduling

    G. Material Requirements Planning

VII. Controlling Operations

    A. Cost Control

    B. Purchasing Control

        1. Building Close Links with Suppliers

        2. Inventory Ordering Systems

    C. Maintenance Control

    D. Quality Control

VIII. Current Issues in Operations Management

    A. Technology and Product Development

    B. Implementing TQM Successfully

        1. For Lower-Performing Firms

        2. For Medium-Performing Firms

        3. For Higher-Performing Firms

    C. Reducing Inventories

    D. Manufacturer-Supplier Partnerships

E. Flexibility as a Competitive Advantage

F. Speed as a Competitive Advantage

Key Words

Operations Management - The design, operation, and control of the transformation process that converts resources into finished goods and services.

Productivity - The overall output of goods and services produced, divided by the inputs needed to generate that output.

Manufacturing organizations - Organizations that produce physical goods such as steel, automobiles, textiles, and farm machinery.

Service organizations - Organizations that produce nonphysical outputs such as educational, medical, and transportation services that are intangible, can't be stored in inventory, and incorporate the customer of client in the actual production process.

Deindustrialization - The conversion of an economy from dominance by manufacturing to dominance by service-oriented businesses.

Capacity planning - Assessing an operating system's ability to produce a desired number of output units for each type of product during a given time period.

Facilities location planning - The design and location of an operations facility.

Process planning - Determining how a product or service will be produced.

Facilities layout planning - Assessing and selecting among alternative layout options for equipment and workstations.

Process layout - Arranging manufacturing components together according to similarity of function.

Product layout - Arranging manufacturing components according to the progressive steps by which a product is made.

Fixed-position layout - A manufacturing layout in which the product stays in place while tools, equipment, and human skills are brought to it..

Aggregate planning - Planning overall production activities and their associated operating resources.

Master schedule - A schedule that specifies quantity and type of items to be produced; how, when, and where they should be produced; labor force levels; and inventory.

Materials requirements planning (MRP) - A system that dissects products into the materials and parts necessary for purchasing, inventorying, and priority-planning purposes.

Cost center - A unit in which managers are held responsible for all associate costs.

Direct costs - Costs incurred in proportion to the output of a particular good or service.

Indirect costs - Costs that are largely unaffected by changes in output.

Fixed-point reordering system - A system that "flags" the fact that inventory needs to be replenished when it reaches a certain level.

Fixed-interval reordering system - A system that uses time as the determining factor for reviewing and reordering inventory items.

ABC system - A priority system for monitoring inventory items.

Preventive maintenance - Maintenance performed before a breakdown occurs.

Remedial maintenance - Maintenance that calls for the overhaul, replacement, or repair of equipment when it breaks down.

Conditional maintenance - Maintenance that calls for an overhaul or repair in response to an inspection.

Acceptance sampling - A quality control procedure in which a sample is taken and a decision to accept or reject a complete lot is based on a calculation of sample risk error.

Process control - A quality control procedure in which sampling is done during the transformation process to determine whether the process itself is under control.

Attribute sampling - A quality control technique that classifies items as acceptable on the basis of a comparison to a standard.

Variable sampling - A quality control technique in which a measurement is taken to determine how much an item varies from the standard.

Computer-integrated manufacturing (CIM) - Combines the organization's strategic business plan and manufacturing plan with state-of-the-art computer applications.

Flexible manufacturing systems - Systems in which custom-made products can be mass produced by means of computer-aided design, engineering, and manufacturing.

MULTIPLE CHOICE QUESTIONS

1. Which of the following is not true for operations management?

    a. Inputs in operations systems include people, capital, equipment, and materials.
    b. Every organization needs an operations management system.
    c. Operations management refers to the design, operation, and control of raw materials into finished goods and services.
    d. Service organizations are not concerned with operations management.

2. Which is not true for productivity?

    a. Productivity is outputs divided by inputs needed to generate the output.
    b. Productivity can be improved by dealing with larger numbers of suppliers.
    c. For individual companies, increased productivity means a more competitive cost structure.
    d. Productivity is a composite of people and operations variables.

3. _____ begins with a forecast of sales demand.

    a. Capacity planning
    b. Facilities location planning
    c. Process planning
    d. Facilities layout planning

4. Some options for _____ are process, product, and fixed-position.

    a. Capacity planning
    b. Facilities location planning
    c. Process planning
    d. Facilities layout planning

5. Considerations for _____ include shipping costs, availability of labor skills, and energy costs.

    a. Capacity planning
    b. Facilities location planning
    c. Process planning
    d. Facilities layout planning

6. A company makes shirts and has departments for cutting, sewing sleeves, sewing fronts/backs, buttons, and pressing. Each department works on batches of items so that the shirts are not made in any particular order, but each department is kept busy each day producing its component part of the shirt. What kind of layout does the company use?

   a. process layout
   b. product layout
   c. fixed-position layout
   d. none of the above.

7. An example of _____ is an assembly line production of cassette players.

   a. process layout
   b. product layout
   c. fixed-position layout
   d. none of the above.

8. _____ specifies the quantity and type of each item to be produced for a period of time.

   a. Aggregate planning
   b. Master Scheduling
   c. Material requirements planning
   d. Capacity planning

9. _____ dissects products into the materials and parts necessary for purchasing, inventory, and priority planning purposes.

   a. Aggregate planning
   b. Master Scheduling
   c. Material requirements planning
   d. Capacity planning

10. During _____ , the best overall production rate to adopt and the overall number of workers needed for a specific time period are determined.

    a. Aggregate planning
    b. Master Scheduling
    c. Material requirements planning
    d. Capacity planning

11. Cost center managers are held responsible for _____ in their units.

    a. direct costs
    b. indirect costs
    c. both direct and indirect costs
    d. neither direct nor indirect costs

12. A priority system for monitoring inventory items is

    a. EOQ.
    b. fixed-interval.
    c. ABC system.
    d. fixed-point reordering system.

13. A technique for balancing purchasing, ordering, carrying, and stockout costs to derive the optimum quantity for a purchase order is

    a. EOQ.
    b. fixed-interval.
    c. ABC system.
    d. fixed-point reordering system.

14. A system that uses time as the determining factor for ordering inventory items is

    a. EOQ.
    b. fixed-interval.
    c. ABC system.
    d. fixed-point reordering system.

15. If a belt breaks and while it is being repaired workers notice that some saws need to be sharpened, this illustrates

    a. conditional maintenance.
    b. preventive maintenance.
    c. remedial maintenance.
    d. none of the above.

16. An example of _____ is if a production line is suddenly shut down because a belt is broken and must be replaced.

    a. conditional maintenance.
    b. preventive maintenance.
    c. remedial maintenance.
    d. none of the above.

17. Sampling items during the transformation process to see if the transfer process is under control is called

    a. acceptance sampling.
    b. variable sampling.
    c. attribute sampling.
    d. process control.

18. A quality control technique where items are accepted or rejected based on some measurement is called

   a. acceptance sampling.
   b. variable sampling.
   c. attribute sampling.
   d. process control.

19. An examination of some number of materials or products to determine if a lot should be accepted or rejected based on the calculation of sample risk error is called

   a. acceptance sampling.
   b. variable sampling.
   c. attribute sampling.
   d. process control.

20. If the entire manufacturing process from order entry to order shipping is computerized, it is a

   a. CAD.
   b. CIM.
   c. CAM.
   d. JIT.

TRUE/FALSE QUESTIONS

1. T F   Every organization has an operations system that creates value by transforming inputs into outputs.

2. T F   To improve productivity, management needs to focus on operations variables, not people.

3. T F   Manufacturing organizations dominate in the U.S. today.

4. T F   Deindustrialization is the conversion of an economy from dominance by manufacturing to dominance by service-oriented businesses.

5. T F   It is harder to improve productivity in a manufacturing organization than a service organization because fewer factors are under management's control.

6. T F   Four key decisions (capacity, location, process, and layout) provide the long-term strategic direction for operations planning.

7. T F   A master schedule is a type of long-term plan.

8. T F   Capacity planning is determining how a product or service will be produced.

9. T F   A process layout is arranging manufacturing components according to the progressive steps by which a product is made.

10. T F   Material requirements planning is planning overall production activities and their associated operating resources.

11. T F   A rapidly growing trend in manufacturing is turning suppliers into partners.

12. T F   The objective of EOQ is to balance the costs associated with inventories: carrying costs, purchasing costs, stockout costs, and ordering costs.

13. T F   A fixed-interval reordering system is a system that "flags" the fact that inventory needs to be replenished when it reaches a certain level.

14. T F   Quality should be designed into the product in the manufacturing process.

15. T F   Computer-aided manufacturing (CAM) and computer-aided design (CAD) are typically the basis for computer integrated manufacturing (CIM).

MATCH TERMS WITH DEFINITIONS

a. Process control
b. Operations management
c. ABC system
d. Materials requirements planning (MRP)
e. Computer-integrated manufacturing (CIM)
f. Fixed-position layout
g. Master schedule
h. Attribute sampling
i. Variable sampling
j. Acceptance sampling
k. Cost center
l. Fixed-interval reordering system
m. Process layout
n. Productivity
o. Flexible manufacturing systems

___ 1. The design, operation, and control of the transformation process that converts resources into finished goods and services.

___ 2. The overall output of goods and services produced, divided by the inputs needed to generate that output.

___ 3. Arranging manufacturing components together according to similarity of function.

___ 4. A manufacturing layout in which the product stays in place while tools, equipment, and human skills are brought to it..

___ 5. A schedule that specifies quantity and type of items to be produced; how, when, and where they should be produced; labor force levels; and inventory.

___ 6. A system that dissects products into the materials and parts necessary for purchasing, inventorying, and priority-planning purposes.

___ 7. A unit in which managers are held responsible for all associate costs.

___ 8. A system that uses time as the determining factor for reviewing and reordering inventory items.

___ 9. A priority system for monitoring inventory items.

___ 10. A quality control procedure in which a sample is taken and a decision to accept or reject a complete lot is based on a calculation of sample risk error.

___ 11. A quality control technique that classifies items as acceptable on the basis of a comparison to a standard.

___ 12. A quality control technique in which a measurement is taken to determine how much an item varies from the standard.

___ 13. Combines the organization's strategic business plan and manufacturing plan with state-of-the-art computer applications.

___ 14. Systems in which custom-made products can be mass produced by means of computer-aided design, engineering, and manufacturing.

___ 15. A quality control procedure in which sampling is done during the transformation process to determine whether the process itself is under control.

CHAPTER 20

CONTROL TOOLS AND TECHNIQUES

Chapter Objectives

1. Describe the four directions in which organizational communication can flow.

2. Identify five common communication networks.

3. Explain the purpose of a management information system (MIS).

4. Differentiate between data and information.

5. Outline the key elements in designing an MIS.

6. Explain how MIS is changing the manager's job and communications in organizations.

7. Describe how budgets are used as control tools.

8. Explain what the various financial ratios measure.

9. Describe TQM control charts.

10. Explain how to determine the most economic order quantity.

11. Identify six performance appraisal methods.

12. List behaviors related to effective disciplining.

13. Describe the organizational factors that serve as indirect behavioral controls.

Chapter Outline

I. Information Controls

    A. Organizational Communication

        1. Formal Versus Informal Communication

2. Direction of Communication Flow

   a. Downward

   b. Upward

   c. Lateral

   d. Diagonal

3. Communication Networks

   a. Five Common Networks

   b. Evaluation of Network Effectiveness

   c. An Informal Network: The Grapevine

B. Information Systems

   1. What is a Management Information System?

   2. How are Information Systems Used in Controlling?

   3. Designing the MIS

      a. Analyze the Decision System

      b. Analyze information requirements

      c. Aggregate the decisions

      d. Design information processing

   4. Implementing the MIS

      a. Pretest the System Before Installation

      b. Prepare Users with Proper Training

      c. Prepare for Resistance

      d. Get Users Involved

      e. Check for Security

      f. Build in Regular Reviews

5. How MISs are Changing the Manager's Job

   a. Hands-on Involvement

   b. Decision-Making Capability

   c. Organization Design

   d. Power

6. How MISs are Changing Organizational Communication

   a. Patterns of Communication Flow Will Change

   b. Communication Overload Should Be Lessened

   c. Face-to-Face Communication will Take on a More Symbolic Role

II. Financial Controls

   A. Budgets Revisited

   B. Ratio Analysis

III. Operations Controls

   A. TQM Control Charts

   B. EOQ Model

IV. Behavioral Controls

   A. Direct Supervision

   B. Performance Appraisal

      1. Written Essays

      2. Critical Incidents

      3. Graphic Rating Scales

      4. Behaviorally Anchored Rating Scales

      5. Multiperson Comparison

      6. Objectives

7. New Approaches to Performance Appraisal

8. Providing Feedback in the Appraisal Review

9. Performance Appraisal in Other Countries

C. Discipline

1. The "Hot Stove" Rule of Discipline

    a. Immediacy

    b. Advance Warning

    c. Consistency

    d. Impersonal nature

2. Developing Effective Discipline Skills

    a. Confront Employee in a Calm, Objective, Serious Manner

    b. State the Problem Specifically

    c. Keep the Discussion Impersonal

    d. Allow the Employee to Explain His or Her Position

    e. Maintain Control of the Discussion

    f. Obtain agreement on How Mistakes Can Be Prevented

    g. Select Disciplinary Action Progressively

3. More Serious Employee Behavior Problems

D. Substitutes for Direct Control

1. Selection Process

2. Organizational Culture

3. Degree of Formalization

4. Employee Training

Key Words

Organizational communication - The flow of information within the organization throughout the various channels and networks.

> **Formal communication** - Communication that follows the authority chain of command or that's necessary to do a job.
>
> **Informal communication** - Communication that is not approved by management and not defined by the structural hierarchy.
>
> **Downward communication** - Communication that flows from a manager down the authority hierarchy.
>
> **Upward communication** - Communication that flows from subordinates to higher-level managers.
>
> **Lateral communication** - Communication among any horizontally equivalent personnel.
>
> **Diagonal communication** - Communication that cuts across functions and levels in an organization.

Communication networks - Vertical and horizontal communication patterns.

Grapevine - The informal communication network.

Management information system (MIS) - A system that provides management with needed information on a regular basis.

Data - Raw, unanalyzed facts.

Information - Analyzed and processed data.

Control charts - A management control tool that show results over a period of time, with statistically determined upper and lower limits.

Economic order quantity (EOQ) - A technique for balancing purchase, ordering, carrying, and stockout costs to derive the optimum quantity for a purchase order.

Performance appraisal - The evaluation of an individual's work performance in order to arrive at objective personnel decisions.

> **Written essay** - A performance appraisal technique in which an evaluator writes out a description of an employee's strengths, weaknesses, past performance, and potential, and then makes suggestions for improvement.

Critical incidents - A performance appraisal technique in which an evaluator lists key behaviors that separate effective from ineffective job performance.

Graphic rating scales - A performance appraisal technique in which an evaluator rates a set of performance factors on an incremental scale.

Behaviorally anchored rating scales (BARS) - A performance appraisal technique in which an evaluator rates employees on specific job behaviors derived from performance dimensions.

Multiperson comparisons - A performance appraisal technique in which individuals are compared to one another.

Group order ranking - A performance appraisal approach that groups employees into ordered classifications.

Individual ranking - A performance appraisal approach that ranks employees in order from highest to lowest.

Paired comparison - A performance appraisal approach in which each employee is compared to every other employee and rated as either the superior or weaker member of the pair.

360 degree feedback - A performance appraisal review that uses feedback from supervisors, subordinates, and co-workers -- the full circle of people with whom the manager interacts.

Discipline - Actions taken by a manager to enforce the organization's standards and regulations.

"Hot stove" rule - Discipline should immediately follow an infraction, provide ample warning, be consistent, and impersonal.

Employee assistance programs (EAPs) - Company-sponsored programs whose goal is to help employees adjust to and overcome personal problems that are adversely affecting their workplace performance.

MULTIPLE CHOICE QUESTIONS

1. Which is not true for an MIS?

    a. MIS is a system that provides management with needed information on a regular basis.
    b. The MIS provides a system of order, arrangement, and purpose.
    c. MIS is a computer based system.
    d. MIS focuses on providing management with information, not just data.

2. Informal communication is

    a. not defined by a structural hierarchy.
    b. another term for the "grapevine".
    c. is communication that is not approved by management.
    d. all of the above.

3. _____ is communication among members of work groups, among managers, or among any horizontally equivalent persons.

    a. Downward communication
    b. Upward communication
    c. Lateral communication
    d. Diagonal communication

4. _____ flows from a manager through the chain of command to lower level workers.

    a. Downward communication
    b. Upward communication
    c. Lateral communication
    d. Diagonal communication

5. _____ cuts across functions and levels in the organization.

    a. Downward communication
    b. Upward communication
    c. Lateral communication
    d. Diagonal communication

6. _____ flows from subordinates to higher level managers.

    a. Downward communication
    b. Upward communication
    c. Lateral communication
    d. Diagonal communication

7. The _____ communication network allows members to interact with an adjoining member, but no further.

    a. chain
    b. Y
    c. wheel
    d. circle

8. The _____ communication network has direct line authority relationships with no deviation.

    a. chain
    b. Y
    c. wheel
    d. circle

9. The _____ communication network is used when fast communication is needed and there is a definite leader.

    a. chain
    b. Y
    c. wheel
    d. circle

10. The _____ is used when high accuracy and moderate speed are needed and there is a leader with some power.

    a. chain
    b. Y
    c. wheel
    d. circle

11. The most popular grapevine pattern is the

    a. single strand.
    b. cluster.
    c. gossip.
    d. probability.

12. Which is not a use for performance appraisals?

    a. personnel research
    b. making orientation decisions
    c. identify training needs
    d. input for human resource planning

13. In the _____ method, each employee is compared to every other employee and rated as either the superior or weaker member of each comparison group.

    a. critical incident
    b. group order ranking
    c. behaviorally anchored rating scale
    d. paired comparison

14. In the _____ method, an evaluator rates employees on specific job behaviors derived from performance dimensions of the job.

    a. critical incident
    b. group order ranking
    c. behaviorally anchored rating scale
    d. paired comparison

15. This part of the "hot stove" rule is illustrated when a manager disciplines a worker as soon as possible after the rules infraction has taken place.

    a. advance warning
    b. impersonal nature
    c. immediacy
    d. consistency

16. A company's policy manual which states rules and punishments is an example of which part of the "hot stove" rule?

    a. advance warning
    b. impersonal nature
    c. immediacy
    d. consistency

17. Formal performance appraisals of managers are not commonly used in

    a. Japan.
    b. Sweden.
    c. China.
    d. Israel.

18. Managers are sometimes reluctant to give a formal performance appraisal review of each employee because

    a. they lack confidence in the appraisal method.
    b. they fear confrontation with employees.
    c. formal appraisals are time consuming.
    d. all of the above.

19. Operations control includes all but one of the following

    a. monitor production schedule to ensure it is on schedule.
    b. assess proper quality and quantity of supplies purchased.
    c. evaluate employees through performance appraisals.
    d. make sure equipment is well maintained.

20. All but one of the following are steps in designing the MIS.

    a. Analyze the decision system.
    b. Analyze information requirement.
    c. Write the appropriate software.
    d. Design information processing.

TRUE/FALSE QUESTIONS

1. T F   The term "system" in MIS implies order, arrangement, and purpose.

2. T F   Information is raw, unanalyzed facts.

3. T F   The MIS system must be regularly modified and updated if it is to give the organization a sustainable, competitive advantage.

4. T F   Lateral communication is used to inform, direct, coordinate, and evaluate subordinates.

5. T F   The circle network does not allow work group members to interact.

6. T F   If speed of communication is important, the circle and chain networks are preferred.

7. T F   The grapevine is an informal network for communication.

8. T F   In a highly authoritative environment, upward communication still takes place, but it is limited to the managerial ranks and to providing control information to upper management.

9. T F   Since managers have become end-users, data processing professionals have had to switch from providing managers with information to helping them get their own information.

10. T F   According to the "hot stove" rule, the best channel for organization communication is written communication.

200

11. T F   In administering discipline, managers should be loose, informal, and relaxed.

12. T F   A behaviorally anchored rating scale is a performance appraisal technique in which an evaluator lists key behaviors that separate effective from ineffective job performance.

13. T F   It is not important for managers to review an employee's performance appraisal with him/her.

14. T F   Evidence indicates that acquiring a mentor who is part of the organization power core is essential for managers who aspire to make to the top.

15. T F   As long as process variables fall within an acceptable range, the system is said to be "in control".

MATCH TERMS WITH DEFINITIONS

a. Performance appraisal
b. Information
c. Control charts
d. Critical incidents
e. Communication networks
f. Graphic rating scales
g. Organizational communication
h. Behaviorally anchored rating scales (BARS)
i. Data
j. "Hot stove" rule
k. Economic order quantity
l. Lateral communication
m. 360 degree feedback
n. Group order ranking
o. Diagonal communication

____ 1. The flow of information within the organization throughout the various channels and networks.

____ 2. Communication among any horizontally equivalent personnel.

____ 3. A performance appraisal review that uses feedback from supervisors, subordinates, and co-workers -- the full circle of people with whom the manager interacts.

____ 4. Communication that cuts across functions and levels in an organization.

___ 5. Raw, unanalyzed facts.

___ 6. A performance appraisal approach that groups employees into ordered classifications.

___ 7. A technique for balancing purchase, ordering, carrying, and stockout costs to derive the optimum quantity for a purchase order.

___ 8. A performance appraisal technique in which an evaluator lists key behaviors that separate effective from ineffective job performance.

___ 9. A management control tool that show results over a period of time, with statistically determined upper and lower limits.

___ 10. Vertical and horizontal communication patterns.

___ 11. A performance appraisal technique in which an evaluator rates a set of performance factors on an incremental scale.

___ 12. A performance appraisal technique in which an evaluator rates employees on specific job behaviors derived from performance dimensions.

___ 13. Analyzed and processed data.

___ 14. Discipline should immediately follow an infraction, provide ample warning, be consistent, and impersonal.

___ 15. The evaluation of an individual's work performance in order to arrive at objective personnel decisions.

ANSWERS TO OBJECTIVE QUESTIONS

CHAPTER 1

Multiple Choice

1. b   2. d   3. c   4. d   5. c   6. c   7. d   8. a   9. d
10. a 11. d 12. b 13. a 14. b 15. d 16. b
17. d 18. c 19. a 20. a

True/False

1. T   2. T   3. F   4. T   5. F   6. F   7. F   8. F
9. T   10. F 11. F 12. F 13. T 14. T 15. F

Matching

1. j   2. h   3. c   4. b   5. g   6. l   7. k   8. i
9. f   10. e 11. a 12. d

CHAPTER 2

Multiple Choice

1. b   2. c   3. a   4. d   5. b   6. c   7. c   8. d
9. c   10. b 11. a 12. c 13. b 14. c 15. d 16. d
17. d 18. a 19. b 20. d

True/False

1. T   2. F   3. F   4. T   5. T   6. T   7. T   8. F
9. F   10. T 11. T 12. T 13. F 14. T 15. F

Matching

1. j   2. c   3. i   4. e   5. g   6. a   7. b   8. m
9. h   10. d 11. l 12. f 13. k

CHAPTER 3

Multiple Choice

1. b   2. c   3. a   4. b   5. a   6. c   7. b   8. c
9. a   10. a 11. d 12. c 13. a 14. a 15. c 16. d
17. a 18. d 19. b 20. c

True/False

1. T   2. T   3. F   4. F   5. T   6. F   7. T   8. F
9. F   10. T 11. T 12. F 13. T 14. T 15. F

Matching

1. d   2. f   3. c   4. e   5. h   6. g   7. b   8. a

CHAPTER 4

Multiple Choice

1. a   2. d   3. a   4. c   5. d   6. a   7. b   8. d
9. b   10. c   11. c   12. d   13. d   14. a   15. d   16. b
17. d   18. d   19. c   20. d

True/False

1. F   2. T   3. F   4. T   5. F   6. T   7. T   8. F
9. F   10. F   11. T   12. T   13. F   14. T   15. T

Matching

1. f   2. c   3. j   4. m   5. d   6. g   7. l   8. b
9. a   10. h   11. k   12. i   13. e

CHAPTER 5

Multiple Choice

1. b   2. d   3. a   4. d   5. a   6. b   7. c   8. a
9. d   10. a   11. b   12. c   13. b   14. a   15. b   16. a
17. d   18. d   19. d   20. d

True/False

1. F   2. T   3. T   4. F   5. F   6. F   7. F   8. T
9. T   10. T   11. F   12. F   13. T   14. F   15. F

Matching

1. f   2. e   3. h   4. j   5. l   6. g   7. k   8. n
9. i   10. o   11. p   12. b   13. a   14. c   15. q   16. d
17. m

CHAPTER 6

Multiple Choice

1. c   2. b   3. d   4. c   5. a   6. c   7. b   8. c
9. a   10. c   11. b   12. a   13. d   14. a   15. c   16. b
17. c   18. d   19. b   20. a

True/False

1. F   2. T   3. T   4. F   5. T   6. T   7. F   8. T
9. T   10. T   11. F   12. T   13. F   14. T   15. F

Matching

1. j   2. f   3. i   4. e   5. n   6. g   7. m   8. h
9. l   10. k   11. a   12. o   13. b   14. c   15. d

CHAPTER 7

Multiple Choice

1. d   2. b   3. d   4. a   5. a   6. c   7. b   8. c
9. a   10. b   11. a   12. b   13. a   14. c   15. d   16. b
17. d   18. c   19. d   20. d

True/False

1. F   2. T   3. T   4. F   5. T   6. F   7. T   8. T
9. F   10. T   11. F   12. T   13. T   14. F   15. T

Matching

1. c   2. f   3. g   4. d   5. h   6. j   7. o   8. k
9. e   10. b   11. n   12. l   13. a   14. m   15. i

CHAPTER 8

Multiple Choice

1. c   2. d   3. d   4. a   5. a   6. c   7. c   8. a
9. c   10. d   11. a   12. b   13. c   14. d   15. b   16. b
17. a   18. c   19. b   20. d

True/False

1. F   2. T   3. F   4. F   5. F   6. T   7. F   8. F
9. F   10. T   11. T   12. F   13. F   14. F   15. T

Matching

1. a   2. d   3. f   4. e   5. l   6. m   7. n   8. o
9. k   10. i   11. j   12. h   13. g   14. c   15. b

CHAPTER 9

Multiple Choice

1. d   2. c   3. b   4. d   5. b   6. d   7. a   8. a
9. c   10. c   11. b   12. b   13. b   14. d   15. a   16. c
17. a   18. b   19. c   20. b

True/False

1. T   2. T   3. F   4. T   5. F   6. F   7. F   8. F
9. T   10. F   11. T   12. F   13. T   14. F   15. F

Matching

1. i   2. k   3. h   4. n   5. c   6. e   7. g   8. b
9. m   10. a   11. f   12. l   13. o   14. d   15. j

CHAPTER 10

Multiple Choice

1. b   2. c   3. c   4. a   5. a   6. a   7. b   8. d
9. c   10. c 11. b 12. b 13. c 14. b 15. d 16. c
17. b 18. c 19. b 20. c

True/False

1. F   2. T   3. T   4. T   5. F   6. T   7. F   8. T
9. F   10. F 11. T 12. T 13. F 14. T 15. T

Matching

1. c   2. j   3. f   4. d   5. h   6. e   7. i   8. a
9. k   10. b 11. m 12. g 13. n 14. o 15. l

CHAPTER 11

Multiple Choice

1. d   2. a   3. c   4. b   5. c   6. d   7. a   8. d
9. a   10. c 11. b 12. c 13. a 14. d 15. b 16. c
17. b 18. a 19. c 20. d

True/False

1. T   2. F   3. F   4. F   5. T   6. T   7. F   8. F
9. F   10. F 11. T 12. F 13. T 14. T 15. T

Matching

1. g   2. m   3. h   4. i   5. e   6. o   7. d   8. b
9. j   10. k 11. c 12. f 13. l 14. a 15. n

CHAPTER 12

Multiple Choice

1. a   2. d   3. b   4. b   5. c   6. d   7. d   8. c
9. c   10. d 11. c 12. d 13. b 14. c 15. b 16. b
17. d 18. a 19. b 20. c

True/False

1. T   2. T   3. F   4. F   5. F   6. T   7. F   8. T
9. F   10. F 11. T 12. T 13. F 14. T 15. F

Matching

1. c   2. e   3. f   4. k   5. l   6. i   7. h   8. b
9. j   10. m 11. g 12. a 13. d

CHAPTER 13

Multiple Choice

1. d   2. b   3. a   4. b   5. d   6. c   7. d   8. b
9. c   10. d 11. b 12. a 13. b 14. c 15. d 16. c
17. d 18. c 19. a 20. d

True/False

1. T   2. T   3. F   4. F   5. F   6. T   7. T   8. F
9. T   10. T 11. F 12. F 13. F 14. F 15. T

Matching

1. g   2. d   3. e   4. h   5. l   6. m   7. g   8. n
9. k   10. r 11. o 12. q 13. p 14. i 15. j 16. c
17. b 18. a

CHAPTER 14

Multiple Choice

1. b   2. a   3. c   4. d   5. c   6. b   7. d   8. a
9. d   10. c 11. c 12. d 13. d 14. d 15. d 16. d
17. b 18. a 19. d 20. b

True/False

1. T   2. F   3. F   4. T   5. T   6. T   7. F   8. T
9. T   10. T 11. T 12. F 13. T 14. T 15. T

Matching

1. a   2. j   3. e   4. p   5. o   6. k   7. l   8. m
9. q   10. n 11. i 12. c 13. d 14. h 15. g 16. b
17. f

CHAPTER 15

Multiple Choice

1. b   2. c   3. d   4. d   5. c   6. c   7. d   8. b
9. b   10. c 11. d 12. c 13. b 14. a 15. c 16. a
17. d 18. b 19. a 20. b

True/False

1. T   2. T   3. F   4. F   5. T   6. T   7. T   8. F
9. T   10. F 11. F 12. F 13. T 14. F 15. F

Matching

1. d   2. h   3. k   4. i   5. j   6. t   7. o   8. s
9. p   10. q 11. n 12. m 13. d 14. l 15. g 16. f
17. e 18. b 19. a 20. c

CHAPTER 16

Multiple Choice

1. b   2. c   3. b   4. d   5. b   6. a   7. c   8. c
9. c   10. d   11. b   12. a   13. c   14. a   15. d   16. a
17. c   18. b   19. d   20. b

True/False

1. F   2. T   3. F   4. T   5. T   6. F   7. T   8. F
9. T   10. T   11. F   12. F   13. F   14. T   15. F

Matching

1. d   2. f   3. e   4. h   5. g   6. o   7. i   8. c
9. j   10. a   11. b   12. n   13. k   14. l   15. m

CHAPTER 17

Multiple Choice

1. c   2. b   3. a   4. a   5. b   6. d   7. d   8. a
9. c   10. d   11. c   12. a   13. c   14. d   15. b   16. b
17. c   18. d   19. a   20. c

True/False

1. T   2. F   3. F   4. T   5. T   6. F   7. T   8. T
9. T   10. F   11. T   12. T   13. T   14. F   15. F

Matching

1. d   2. j   3. e   4. f   5. m   6. n   7. h   8. b
9. o   10. l   11. g   12. a   13. i   14. k   15. c

CHAPTER 18

Multiple Choice

1. c   2. b   3. c   4. b   5. a   6. d   7. d   8. a
9. b   10. d   11. d   12. a   13. c   14. d   15. a   16. c
17. d   18. d   19. a   20. d

True/False

1. T   2. F   3. F   4. F   5. T   6. F   7. T   8. T
9. T   10. F   11. F   12. F   13. T   14. F   15. T

Matching

1. e   2. i   3. l   4. k   5. c   6. d   7. a   8. h
9. b   10. g   11. j   12. f

CHAPTER 19

Multiple Choice

1. d   2. b   3. a   4. d   5. b   6. b   7. b   8. b
9. c   10. a   11. a   12. c   13. a   14. b   15. a   16. c
17. d   18. d   19. a   20. b

True/False

1. T   2. F   3. F   4. T   5. F   6. T   7. F   8. F
9. F   10. F   11. T   12. T   13. F   14. T   15. T

Matching

1. b   2. n   3. m   4. f   5. g   6. d   7. k   8. l
9. c   10. j   11. h   12. i   13. e   14. o   15. a

CHAPTER 20

Multiple Choice

1. c   2. d   3. c   4. a   5. d   6. b   7. d   8. a
9. c   10. b   11. b   12. b   13. d   14. c   15. c   16. a
17. b   18. d   19. d   20. c

True/False

1. T   2. F   3. T   4. F   5. F   6. F   7. T   8. T
9. T   10. T   11. F   12. F   13. F   14. T   15. T

Matching

1. g   2. l   3. m   4. o   5. i   6. n   7. k   8. d
9. c   10. e   11. f   12. h   13. b   14. j   15. a